ADVENTUROUS LIVES, DARING ACTS

True Stories of the Famous and the Forgotten

BY JIM HOLDEN

VAL DE GRÂCE
BOOKS

Val de Grace Books
Napa, California

ISBN: 978-0-9848849-7-1
Library of Congress Control Number: 2021946402

Cover design by Melissa Holden
Book interior by Dorothy Carico Smith

To Mary,
who has helped me soar
and kept me grounded for over fifty years

ALSO BY JIM HOLDEN

It Happened in Marin

—CONTENTS—

NOTE TO READERS

The stories in this book feature adventure, daring, and passion. All are true.

One recounts a free climb of a three-hundred-foot redwood and the beginning of a new realm of study. A second portrays Ishi, the last unconquered Native American, as he emerges from the wild into twentieth century California and later returns briefly to the wild. In another, we ride the air with the last wild California condor and join in the rescue of condors from the oblivion of extinction.

We capture John Steinbeck's raw emotions during a period of his making and undoing. We live the cruel youth of Bill Graham and accompany him and rock 'n' roll into the sixties. We break out of San Quentin and other prisons with America's premier escape artist.

We spend time with Jack London and tap into his hunger for a life chock-full of adventure. We visit the Chez Panisse kitchen with Alice Waters and watch as she and others change the food culture of America. We relax with John Muir and President Theodore Roosevelt around a campfire and listen far into the night. We witness Christo's daring creation of a twenty-four-mile fence in defiance of authorities.

Several of the stories touch on preservation and the land. In all of them we experience adventure and audacity.

Lives are enclosed between the ports of call of birth and death. But in some there are peak periods where all hangs in the balance, hard choices are made, and daring acts performed.

In this book I recount these times of total engagement—some in the lives of the famous and some in the lives of those forgotten or only vaguely remembered. All lived their passion. I have tried to capture it for the readers of this book. I hope I have succeeded.

—Jim Holden

"What it boils down to is that everything exists,
it is what you pick out of the grab bag of experience that matters."

—*John Steinbeck*

A New Realm
of Wonder

A NEW REALM OF WONDER

In 1987, on an impulse, Steve Sillett made the first free climb of a redwood standing over three hundred feet tall. Because it soared skyward a long way before there was any hint of a branch, he had to reach it by way of a shorter redwood nearby. So Steve climbed the shorter redwood to a branch near its top, far above the death zone of fifty feet from which a fall is fatal.

Standing on the branch, which trembled under his weight, he calculated his odds of successfully leaping, grabbing, and holding on to a branch extending from the taller redwood. Since he was without ropes or other safety equipment, it was a life-or-death matter. He would be leaping from an unsteady perch and attempting to catch the end of a branch that would bend sharply under his weight when he grabbed it. Steve didn't look down.

He took a breath, crouched, and jumped. His hands grasped the taller redwood's extended branch, and he gripped it tightly while he bounced up and down, his feet swinging below. He took another breath and, hanging from the branch, traversed hand by hand toward the tree's trunk and a secure position. Once he got to the trunk, he grabbed a branch above, swung himself up, and stood. He called out to his companion, Marwood Harris, to come up and join him.

Standing there waiting, Sillett was unaware that this climb would ultimately determine his life's course and open up a new area of scientific exploration and study. For now, all that mattered was his next move.

Harris followed Sillett's lead, leaping from the shorter tree to the taller one. He was greeted by a swarm of yellow jackets stinging his face, neck, and hands. He concentrated on ignoring them and made his way hand by hand to the trunk, then swatted angrily at them. Sillett climbed higher to escape, Harris followed, and soon they were free of their attackers.

They continued their ascent until Sillett stopped at a twelve-foot gap between branches. He would have to climb about six feet of trunk before he could grab hold of the next branch. He was ninety feet up and still more than two hundred feet below the top. He pushed aside a wave of fear and focused on cramming his fingers and the toes of his shoes deep into the thick bark furrows. Shinnying and reaching, he made his way up, grabbed the branch above and swung his leg over it. He was still in the lower half of the tree.

Sillett and Harris were climbing both height and time. It takes about six hundred years for a redwood to grow from a seed to a large tree and another two hundred or so for it to reach maturity. At some point, the top of the tree, its leader, falls off. Then the tree sends out new trunks from its large limbs, and these new trunks grow vertically, paralleling the main trunk. Over centuries, they grow new branches that in turn send up new trunks, and the process repeats itself. The crowns of the largest redwoods contain a multitude of trunks and branches that overlap and buttress each other to form the canopy.

Sillett and Harris continued upward and entered the canopy's layer upon layer of green. They could see nothing below or above—they were surrounded by green.

Sillett was then a junior at Portland's Reed College. He had graduated from high school in three years with straight A's, gone to community college for a year, and then transferred to Reed with a full scholarship. He had started to climb trees around campus as a break from his studies. Harris and a few others would sometimes join Sillett in the treetops where they talked, read, and relaxed. Sillett told Harris that if it weren't for tree climbing and Dungeons & Dragons, he wasn't sure he would have remained in college.

Up high in the tall redwood, Sillett was focusing on each move. The canopy was unlike the top of any other tree he had climbed. He was surrounded by an airy garden of mosses, ferns, lichens, huckleberries, and other plants. Lichens had been an interest of Sillett's since childhood, and he tore some off and stuffed them into his shirt pocket.

When and if he got down, he would show them to a botany professor for identification.

The branches of the redwood's canopy were larger than the ones lower down, unlike other trees, whose higher branches are smaller. Sillett and Harris made their way through the canopy. As they neared the top, the sunlight poured through, lighting up the canopy and its airy gardens in limitless shades of green.

On top of the huge platform of green, they looked out over the forest and could see the blue of the Pacific Ocean. The climb had taken them an hour or a little longer.

The top branches were so intertwined and close together that they could generally move about easily. They sat there for a long time, each absorbed in his own thoughts and this new realm of wonder. As the sun began its plunge into the ocean, the threat of darkness forced them into action. The climb down would be scarier than the one up.

On the descent they were forced at least once to drop in free fall for a few feet to grab the next branch down. They reached the gap where they had jumped to the tall redwood and made the heart-stopping leap in reverse to the shorter one. From there they climbed down without incident.

The experience helped Sillett decide that for his senior thesis he would research and write about lichens growing on old growth Douglas firs. For some seven years after his redwood climb, Sillett climbed Douglas firs for his research, but not redwoods.

He used safety equipment and learned sophisticated climbing techniques from high tree arborists. They taught him to use a climbing harness, ropes, and specialized knots that allowed him to move safely and freely both vertically and horizontally and even to sky-walk in midair. Once comfortable with the new techniques, Sillett had complete climbing freedom.

He would use that freedom later to climb the tallest redwoods and explore their canopies and to push into a new area of knowledge. He required only two elements: preserved old-growth forest where the tallest redwoods grow and a fellow to search them out and guide him to the very tallest. The fellow was then unknown to Sillett, but his name was Michael Taylor.

OLD-GROWTH FOREST REDWOODS

REDWOODS ARE THE TALLEST things alive and the second-largest in mass to giant sequoias. Redwoods live naturally within a narrow band along the Northern California coast, in a range extending north from Big Sur to just beyond the California-Oregon border.

Old-growth redwoods are intertwined in both their canopies and their root systems. They are connected by the microclimates they create and by the streams, creeks, and rills of their watershed and all the life within. Some existing redwoods have stood sentinel for two thousand years, more than fifty human generations.

Where redwoods exist in numbers, they dominate everything, including the soil, other plant life, and even the climate. For eons their height and size, their resistance to fire and insect attack, and their location have protected them against virtually all enemies other than old age.

The enemy from which redwoods have no protection is the human desire for redwood lumber. Before the California gold rush virtually all redwood forests were old-growth forest—that is, largely undisturbed by man. The felling of redwoods for lumber began in earnest with the gold rush and has soared since.

The old-growth redwood forests conceal within their expanse the very tallest redwoods. The problem is that 95 percent of the old-growth redwoods have already been lumbered.

In the San Francisco Bay Area, the old-growth redwoods were all but gone before there was a successful movement for their preservation. California's first state park, Big Basin State Park, was established in 1902 near Santa Cruz to save the old-growth redwoods there. The last significant stand of virgin redwoods in Marin County was protected as Muir Woods National Monument in 1908.

Beginning in the 1920s, the Save the Redwoods League was the leader in protecting redwoods from destruction. It is responsible for the creation of the four California state parks that protect large stands of old-growth redwoods: Humboldt Redwoods, Prairie Creek Redwoods, Del Norte Coast Redwoods, and Jedediah Smith Redwoods state parks.

The initiative for a national park to preserve ancient redwood forests began early in the 1960s with a push by the National Geographic Society. To spur public and political support, its leaders hoped to discover on private land a redwood tall enough break all records. National Geographic hired Paul Zahl to lead an expedition in search of such a tree and to write an article about it.

Zahl and his team explored the area around Redwood Creek on timber company land in Humboldt County. The largest old-growth redwoods were growing on alluvial flats in canyons and valleys carved by the creek, but the vegetation there was so thick that it greatly hampered exploration. Zahl's team found no record setters on the expedition.

On a return trip Zahl managed to penetrate the dense vegetation and discovered a tree he estimated to be 370 feet tall. National Geographic brought in a team of surveyors, who measured it at 367.8 feet, the tallest tree then known. They had their record-breaking redwood, their symbol for the public to rally around. In a moment of unrestrained imaginative flair, National Geographic named the grove with the tall tree the "Tall Tree Grove."

In 1968 Congress established California's Redwood National Park, including a narrow 7.5-mile corridor encompassing a lower stretch of Redwood Creek holding the Tall Tree Grove. Conservationists called the narrow appendage the "Worm."

In 1978 Congress widened the Worm to the adjacent ridgetops to better conserve the Tall Tree Grove by protecting some of its watershed. It also expanded the park generally to encompass more old-growth forest.

ENTER MICHAEL TAYLOR

IN THE FALL OF 1986, a young man named Michael Taylor took Redwood National Park's clearly marked, easy walk to the Tall Tree Grove. He was disappointed. He had seen lots of redwood groves, and he was convinced that taller trees grew in unexplored stands of ancient redwood forest. Over time the thought would drift in and out of his brain and finally possess him.

After a short stint in Southern California, he moved back to redwood country. A billionaire's son, Taylor received no financial support and had to fend for himself. He got a job as a checkout clerk at the C&V Market in Eureka and eked out a bare existence. After a while, he began pursuing a passion—almost an obsession—to find the tallest living redwood.

He had an uncanny feel for old growth redwood forest and the elements in them that produced the tallest trees. Still the search, location, and measurement of prospects required great effort and time.

He could not determine the height of a tall redwood from underneath because it was impossible to see through the canopy. He needed to find a vantage point not too far away where he could overlook a promising grove's canopy to select the redwood that towered highest.

There was no certainty that the tree that seemed the tallest to him from afar actually was. And even if he correctly spotted the tallest redwood, the task of locating it in the thick of the forest and measuring it was daunting.

In January of 1994 Taylor climbed a grassy area looking down on some flat areas of Humboldt State Park. He scoped an area about a mile away containing tall redwoods and focused on one rising above the canopy. He named it the "Humboldt Tree" and triangulated it with three compass readings.

For the next three months he bushwhacked through the forest trying to locate it. He used his compass readings and then measured each promising tree, but to no avail. In April he finally found it. The tree leaned over at an angle which made measurement exceedingly difficult and precision from the ground impossible. Taylor measured it as accurately as he could and determined that the Humboldt Tree was roughly 371 feet high, about a foot taller than any other known tree.

Still there was no certainty. The only foolproof method of determining a tall redwood's height was to climb to the top and spool out a weighted line to the ground. And Taylor was not a climber.

Taylor kept the discovery to himself for a while, but that summer he opened up and told an acquaintance, who recounted it to Steve Sillett. Sillett telephoned Taylor, whom he did not know, and after talking to him a while thought that Taylor might be for real. Sillett suggested that he climb the tree and measure it from the top. Taylor offered to take him to it.

In September of 1994 Sillett and his team piled into trucks and drove down from Oregon to meet Taylor and climb the Humboldt Tree. Sillett had been climbing Douglas firs for his research, but he had never forgotten the unexplored world of the canopy in the tall redwood he had climbed years earlier. He was excited at the prospect of climbing another—this time with ropes.

Sillett and his team met Taylor, and he guided them in the gathering darkness to the Humboldt Tree. Its exaggerated lean scared them. The tree seemed likely to fall at any moment. After a serious group discussion Sillett finally said, "I think it'll be fine to climb, as long as it's not too windy tomorrow."

The climbing team downed some trail mix in the dark and went to sleep. Taylor had to leave and drive back to Eureka because he was charged with opening the C&V Market the next morning.

The shape and lean of the Humboldt Tree were unusual. The main trunk of the tree had started leaning centuries before. A new trunk had emerged from its lower part and grown straight up. The group decided to climb the Humboldt Tree's vertical trunk and then by way of ropes make it over to the leaning main trunk.

As lead climber, Sillett was the first to the Humboldt Tree's top. He took a measuring line out of his pack, attached a weighted throw bag to it, and dropped it from the tree's highest point. The line measured the drop at 359 feet. It was not the tallest tree. The team told Taylor the disappointing news later that day when he returned from the market.

The climbers decided to sleep in the tree overnight and fixed their hammocks. A little past midnight they woke to find that a furious storm had swept in. The trunk was bouncing up and down in the wind and vibrating as it leaned down even farther. Each dip produced an ominous sound, seemingly emitted from underneath the base of the tree.

The group debated whether to climb down, but a nighttime descent in a storm seemed more dangerous to them than riding it out in the tree. Fortunately, after a short time the storm had vented its fury, and in the morning, they climbed down safely.

A month or two later Sillett presented a paper at a scientific conference describing the climb and extolling the redwood canopy as a new world for exploration. He returned from the conference to a message from Taylor and returned the call. Taylor told him that the tree they had climbed had just fallen in a storm. Steve drove to Eureka and met Taylor at the C&V Market. They hiked in to see the fallen tree.

The prostrate trunk was sixteen feet high, almost three times their own height. It had smashed a smaller redwood when it fell, sending chunks of wood and debris in all directions. The tremendous power of the tree's fall had spattered mud sixty feet up the trunks of the surrounding trees. Even prostrate, the tree was awesome.

THE WORLD OF THE CANOPY

SOMETIME LATER SILLETT ASKED Taylor if he knew of any other trees of interest. He did.

In 1991 Taylor had searched Prairie Creek Redwoods State Park for the tallest redwood. One day while in deep, he discovered an unknown dense grove of giants. He didn't know exactly where he was, but by the thumping of his heart he knew he had discovered a grove that was extraordinary. The first tree he measured was huge with four large trunks in its crown. He named the tree "Atlas" and the stand the "Atlas Grove."

In the fall of 1996 Taylor guided Sillett to the grove, which was still known only to Taylor. Sillett was now a professor at Humboldt State University. He had grown to admire Taylor's knowledge and keen memory of the forest, his attentive accuracy, and his intellectual honesty. Taylor was one of the very few people with whom Sillett felt he could communicate on a personal level.

Sillett was intent on studying the redwood canopy, and there was no better place than Taylor's Atlas Grove. Sillett began climbing its giants. He commented to others that Taylor had named the Atlas Grove well. "When you are up in Atlas," he said, "you get this overwhelming sense of a tree holding up the earth."

Sillett wanted to understand the canopy's structure and flow. He enlisted a large team to help him map the entire grove in three dimensions and identify all living things within it. The complexity of the undertaking was almost unimaginable. One of the trees had 220 trunks, each with its own lateral branches. The Atlas project took numerous people with many different specialties years to complete.

Their study revealed several surprises. The canopy hosted a variety of the trees that commonly grow in association with redwoods, but there they were growing in bonsai form from deep pockets of accumulated soil in the canopy's nooks and crannies. The canopy's ferns housed insects found among the ocean's plankton. The forces that carried them to the high redwoods and allowed them to survive there were unknown. Salamanders of a type normally found crawling on the ground were born, reproduced, and lived their entire life cycles high in the redwoods. Many species of lichens and mosses inhabited the canopy.

The canopy was seemingly a world unto itself, but still inextricably connected to the redwoods, the forest, and the entire ecosystem. And through it to the omnipresence of time.

Time is a chameleon. It takes on the coloration of the life to which it is attached. The life of an insect may be counted in days. The life of a redwood is measured in centuries.

Then consider the lichens, those small, crinkly, crusty green things growing on rocks and trees and in redwood canopies. Lichens are a symbiotic combination of fungus paired with green alga or cyanobacteria, which photosynthesize like plant leaves. It is not clear that lichen have natural lifespans. Scientists studying lichen believe that through its fungus, a lichen can live to be several thousand years old or beyond.

Perhaps by measuring lifespans of individual entities, we are literally getting lost in the trees rather than seeing the entire forest. Old growth redwood forests endure for eons if one counts the continuous vitality of the ecosystem. From a human perspective, the ecosystem lasts forever. That is, unless we interfere.

THE TALLEST TREE

IN MAY OF 2008, Sillett and Taylor plunged into Jedediah Smith Redwood State Park's redwoods to search for new champion trees. They low-crawled, climbed, and squeezed their way through the profuse, tangled undergrowth of the park's canyons and valleys. Although both became increasingly tired and hungry, they continued their trek for several hours until they stopped exhausted in a gully clogged with vegetation. They had no idea where they were.

Taylor wanted to go back. Sillett was unrelenting in wanting to continue. With some irony Taylor called Sillett a freaking tree fanatic. After more venting, they calmed down and pushed forward for a couple more hours until Taylor screamed.

Taylor was yelling triumphantly at two enormous redwoods joined at the base with a diameter of some thirty feet. Beyond them was a sight even more astounding, a circular wall of monumental redwoods. Their combined mass was colossal, but one tree was larger than any redwood Sillett and Taylor had ever seen. It was later confirmed to be the largest redwood on earth, its trunk thirty feet in diameter. It was larger at its base than the famous General Sherman giant sequoia, but because it tapered more, its total mass was slightly smaller.

The stand of ancient colossal trees is called the Grove of Titans. Its location is known to just a few who study the grove's ecology.

While Sillett continued working on the Atlas project, Taylor persisted in his search for the world's tallest tree. He had formed a close friendship with Chris Atkins, a redwood enthusiast from Sonoma County, and the two began a quest to find the tallest redwood on the planet.

Such a tree needed optimal conditions to reach its skyscraping height, and Taylor and Atkins understood better than anyone where those might exist. They were successful in finding many tall trees, but they felt they still had not discovered the tallest.

In late 2005 they began exploring certain valleys in Redwood National Park, often making harrowing, exhausting bushwhacking forays into unexplored places in the ancient forest that had been added to the park in its 1978 expansion. In the spring of 2006 Taylor and Atkins, together with Sillett, ventured into a territory so difficult and so fatiguing to explore that it was akin to torture. Their efforts were unrewarded.

In July of 2006 Taylor and Atkins decided to probe an area with such thick undergrowth that it took them seven hours to get to their targeted valley. After the sun disappeared behind a high ridge, they noticed a treetop still catching the sunlight. Using lasers that could gauge a tree's height quite accurately, they measured this one at 375 feet, the tallest redwood then known. The two men embraced, and Taylor exulted to Atkins, "I knew it was here. I dreamed about this tree."

Less than two months later, Taylor and Atkins hiked into another valley of ancient forest in the national park's expansion area and found a tree even taller—by laser 380 feet high. They named it "Hyperion." Sillett climbed it later and measured it precisely at 380.1 feet. It is still, as of this writing, the tallest tree known.

ECOSYSTEM

MUCH OF THIS STORY has focused on individual trees, the tallest or largest redwoods. But they grow in complete ecosystems, in communities of other redwoods and accompanying plants, mosses, and lichens. They contain animals, birds, insects, and microorganisms and also inanimate matter, including soil, vital water, and fog. Singling out individual giant trees is quite helpful for preservation—it provides a focus for the public's interest—but it distracts from the overriding importance of the whole.

Ancient redwoods occupy a special place on this planet. They live in a different realm and know matters of land, community, and time which mankind can barely imagine. For the benefit of generations to come, we need to concentrate more on saving old growth redwood forest and other entire ecosystems. By saving more of them, we can better save the land and the communities of life on our planet.

Note: I relied on Richard Preston's excellent book, *The Wild Trees*, for the underlying facts regarding the discovery, climb, and exploration of the tall redwoods. See "Principal Sources" at the end of this book for it and other sources for the story. The words, musings, and focus are mine.

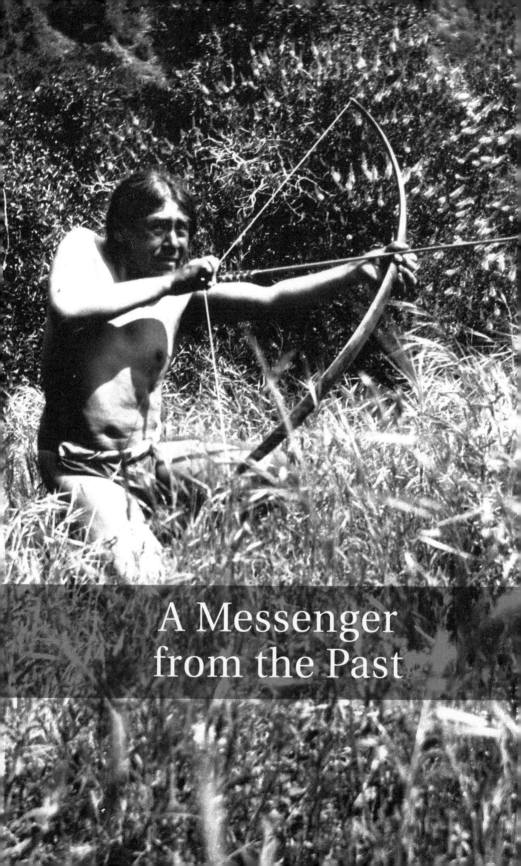

A Messenger
from the Past

A MESSENGER FROM THE PAST

O N AUGUST 29, 1911, the last unconquered Native American walked in from the wild to the outskirts of Oroville, California. He and a small band of his Yahi people had existed sovereign, hidden, and unknown within the borders of the United States for some forty years. They had outlasted the capture of Geronimo and his Apaches by twenty-five years and survived as the country's only free tribe. The man now standing outside a slaughterhouse in Oroville was the last of his people.

His appearance in twentieth-century California defied all settled knowledge. But there he was, exhausted and starving, standing by a slaughterhouse corral. His hair was burnt short as Native Americans in mourning wore it. He carried a small bag containing only a few dried manzanita berries.

The men working at the slaughterhouse were bewildered and uneasy at the sight of him. Not knowing what else to do, they telephoned the sheriff. He arrived quickly with a deputy and took the man to the sheriff's headquarters in Oroville. They housed him in the jail to protect him from the curious gawkers gathered outside.

The man's journey from the wild into twentieth-century America was just beginning. He had departed his world and entered a new age and a new world—one totally unknown to him. It would require far different life skills from those that had sustained him in the past, and whether he could adapt was an open question.

The sheriff gave the man warmed beans with bread and butter, and he devoured them ravenously. While he was eating the beans, the undersheriff offered him a doughnut. The man took the doughnut, examined it carefully, and tentatively tasted a small piece. Then he put the beans aside for a moment and wolfed down the doughnut.

As a test, the sheriff handed him a revolver without cartridges. He did not know how to use it.

No one could verbally communicate with the man until Professor Thomas T. Waterman, an anthropologist from the University of California, arrived by train two days later. Waterman had suspected for a time that a small group of Yana Indians still existed in the wilderness. Upon learning through news reports of the wild man's appearance, he had immediately taken a train to Oroville.

Upon meeting the man, Waterman read to him a phonetic list of Yana words he had brought with him. Disappointingly there was no recognition for a while—until Waterman mouthed the word "siwini," meaning yellow pine, and tapped the jail cot's wooden frame. The man responded with quick recognition and corrected Waterman's pronunciation. Together they repeated "siwini, siwini" several times while banging the frame.

At Waterman's suggestion, the sheriff sent for a Yana Indian named Batwi to see if he could communicate with the man. He was of some help as he and the man spoke related dialects containing some of the same words. Still, communication was difficult.

Waterman obtained permission from the federal Indian Bureau to take the man (soon to be known as "Ishi," though that was not his name) to the building that housed the university's anthropology museum in San Francisco. Ishi was outfitted in modern clothes for the trip but resisted wearing shoes. His bare feet on the ground were his only connection to his former life.

The world Ishi was entering was a total mystery to him except for its hostility. At the train station Ishi was fearful of the incoming locomotive as it belched and smoked its way in. He had never been close to a train although he had seen and heard them from a great distance. Waterman managed to communicate to him that the train could only follow the tracks. Ultimately, Ishi followed Waterman aboard.

That evening they arrived at the museum building in San Francisco, where Ishi would reside in his own apartment on the second floor for the rest of his life. He was now a city dweller, removed from any semblance of his former natural surroundings and life.

In the morning he met the head of the anthropology department, Alfred L. Kroeber, whom he would call his big "chiep" (chief). Over the next few days while everything was strange to Ishi, Kroeber's salient impression of him was his gentleness. Ishi preferred company and was friendly and quietly upbeat. At the same time, he was aware that he was separate. He was one—they were the others.

After Ishi's meeting with Kroeber, Waterman took Ishi across the bay to the university's Berkeley campus and then to his own home for dinner with his wife and two children. In an attempt to adapt to the unfamiliar setting, Ishi imitated the wife's manners at dinner, sometimes so closely that it almost appeared their actions were synchronized.

Reporters demanded to know the wild man's name, and Kroeber felt pressured to give them one. But Ishi remained true to his upbringing and refused to reveal his name for he had been taught to share it only with intimates of his own tribe. Finally, Kroeber chose the name "Ishi" for him, which in the Yana tongue means "man" or "people." Ishi never did disclose his true name.

The Sunday after Ishi's arrival in San Francisco, Kroeber took him through Golden Gate Park to Ocean Beach. At the beach Ishi was far more astounded by the crowd of people than by the ocean's expanse or its crashing waves. He kept repeating in a half whisper, "Hansi saltu, hansi saltu!" Many white people, many white people! It would be a long time before Ishi was comfortable with crowds.

During their tour they passed the museum building several times. Trained to orient himself in new terrain, Ishi would proclaim, "Wo-wi" (my house, my home). At one point he saw a covey of quail take flight. He followed them with his eyes and softly imitated their call.

Ishi now had a name and address. Soon he would have a salaried job as the museum's assistant janitor. He had entered his new life.

THE YAHI AND ISHI'S SURVIVAL

ISHI WAS BORN AROUND 1860 into the Yahi tribe, the southernmost tribe of the Yana people. The Yahi did not mix with the other Yana tribes, and the Yahi language was distinct enough as to prevent meaningful intelligibility between the Yahi and the other Yana tribes.

By the late 1860s, the other Yana people were dead or had been forced on to reservations, pushed aside by the settlers lured to California by the gold rush. The attacks on the Yahi in the foothills of Mt. Lassen were just beginning.

On an August morning in 1865, a man and two women were murdered at a ranch far south of the Yahi homeland. An avenging party of 17 men believed—probably erroneously—that the Yahi were the perpetrators and set up an ambush near one of the largest Yahi villages on Mill Creek. The ambush was successful, and only a few of the Yahi (or "Mill Creeks," as the settlers called them) escaped.

A young child, whom we now know as Ishi, and his mother were among those who did. Ishi remembered the attack but refused to talk about it.

Three years later a group of men tracked and slaughtered another thirty-three Yahi in a cave north of Mill Creek. Two years after that, four men followed Mill Creek upstream to a cave housing some thirty unarmed Yahi, including women, children, and babies. The men covered the cave entrance with their rifles and without remorse killed all of the occupants.

With that massacre the settlers thought they had exterminated the Yahi. They discovered otherwise when they returned to the cave. The bodies of the Yahi had vanished.

The final events leading to the Yahi's long concealment occurred later in 1870. A man named Seagraves discovered several of his cattle missing. He suspected the Yahi and assembled some men to pursue them.

The men caught up with a group of Yahi along Mill Creek. They shot an old man and captured an old woman, a young woman, and a little girl. The remaining Yahi escaped.

Two weeks later, five Yahi men and seven women showed up at Seagraves' cabin. One of the men, whom Seagraves remembered from the recent encounter with the Yahi, made a formal speech to Seagraves. At its conclusion the speaker and four other men presented their bows to him.

Seagraves understood nothing of the speech but assumed that the presentation of the bows was an offer of peace in exchange for the freedom of the female captives taken two weeks earlier. Any decision as to them was up to Hi Good, a local rancher, since they had become his captives. So Seagraves took the Yahi group to Good's cabin.

Good was not at home, but some men were there guarding the captives. While the twelve Yahi and Seagraves waited for Good to return, one of the guards threw a rope over a high tree branch.

At that the Yahi fled in fear and vanished. Their long concealment and stand against civilization had begun. Ishi was then ten years old, or perhaps slightly younger.

For almost four decades there was no contact with the Yahi, although at great intervals some meager evidence of their possible existence would appear. But in 1908 a survey party plotting lines along Deer Creek saw a Native American (whom we now know was Ishi) standing midstream on a rock, fishing spear poised.

The next morning while continuing their survey, the men stumbled upon the Yahi camp. Ishi's sister and an older man fled, but Ishi's partially paralyzed mother was unable to do so.

The surveyors left Ishi's mother alone but robbed the camp of its store of food (primarily acorns and dried salmon), Ishi's bow and quiver of arrows, a wooden drill used to create fire, baskets, moccasins, and tanned hides, among other items. They took everything, leaving the camp inhabitants with nothing.

By the time the survey party returned to the camp after storing away its pilfered contents, Ishi had gathered up his mother and disappeared with her. She died soon after.

Ishi never saw his sister or the older man again. He assumed they had drowned since he could find no trace of them in the homeland they shared and knew so intimately.

Ishi was now without human companions, as well as the objects crucial to survival in the wild. He had no hunting gear, no fire drill, and no baskets for cooking. He may have had a small store of food, for it was the Yahis' practice to stash a portion away from their camp as a safety measure.

Ishi was now truly alone, with no one to help him, no one for comfort, and no one to talk to. Loneliness must have torn at him, and his agony must have been excruciating.

Still, he possessed an incredible ingenuity and vitality that allowed him to survive for three more years alone in the wild. He possessed the character and heart to do it and, in the end, the courage to walk forty miles into the unknown, hostile white world.

ISHI AT THE MUSEUM

ISHI SOMETIMES DEMONSTRATED HIS survival skills at the museum to large crowds, ranging from young school children to curious adults. Everyone watched with interest as he made arrowheads or used the fire drill to create fire.

Ishi's fire drill consisted of (1) the drill, a rounded hardwood stick made of mountain juniper, (2) a softwood base of incense cedar with a gouged-out socket to hold the turning drill, and (3) a short groove notched from the socket to a deposit of dry tinder placed at the groove's end.

To create fire, Ishi placed his knee on the base to hold it steady, clasped the drill between his palms, and twirled it back and forth by alternately sliding one hand forward and the other backwards, as though warming his hands. As he was twirling the drill, he also pressed it downward into the socket. The friction of the drill in the socket produced sawdust and soon charred it. The charred sawdust eventually smoked and then produced a spark that Ishi would blow carefully down the notch onto the tinder. Once the spark ignited the tinder, Ishi would carefully nourish the flame with dried moss and small sticks until it leapt into fire!

With coaching from Ishi, Professor Waterman was able to use the fire drill to produce fire. Flush with success, Waterman announced in one of his classes that to complete the course, each student was required to create fire using the fire drill. He then attempted to demonstrate the technique to the class but failed utterly. He dropped the requirement.

Ishi was not averse to adopting the benefits of civilization. In his new life, he generally admired tools and techniques that would have served him well in his former life. He delighted in matches and thought them far superior to his previous world's fire drill. He also admired glue and adopted it for feathering arrows, joining sinews into bowstrings, and attaching the backing to a bow.

A skilled and precise craftsman, Ishi would watch closely as carpenters worked on a house or woodworkers made a cabinet. From them he adopted the use of a bench vise to hold wood he was fashioning. He considered the vise a vast improvement over his big toe, which formerly had performed the same function. He also greatly appreciated pockets and stuffed them with all sorts of things he wanted to carry with him.

Ishi had three close friends, and a different relationship with each. He looked up to "big chiep" Kroeber as department head. He was close with anthropology professor Waterman and his family and lived with them for a short while.

But Ishi related to Dr. Saxton Pope on a more personal level, and Pope became his closest friend. Their friendship was forged initially by a common interest in archery.

Dr. Pope practiced medicine and was an instructor of surgery at U.C. Medical Center, located adjacent to the university museum. About a year after Ishi's arrival, Pope looked out the window and saw Ishi in the open yard crafting a bow. Pope went outside and watched intently as Ishi worked.

Deciding that he wanted to learn archery from Ishi, a person whose life had depended on his skill with a bow and arrow, he asked Ishi to teach him. That afternoon the two began practicing in an empty meadow and shared their interest in archery for the rest of their lives together.

As their relationship grew, Pope would sometimes bring Ishi into the operating room to watch his surgeries. Ishi was attentive to the procedures and was particularly fascinated by the use and effects of anesthesia. But even after watching several surgeries, the thing that convinced Ishi that Pope was a real doctor was Pope's sleight of hand in making coins vanish and performing other similar magic tricks. Ishi considered his friend "Popey" the most fascinating of his acquaintances.

CAMPING WITH ISHI IN HIS HOMELAND

IN 1914 POPEY, WATERMAN, and Kroeber decided to take Ishi on an extended camping trip to his homeland. Initially Ishi did not want to go, perhaps because he thought it would bring back too many bad memories. But his three friends persisted, and Ishi finally agreed.

Ishi's friends recorded enough about the trip to make it a fascinating window into his past.

For Ishi, the camping trip brought him back into his old world. He had never achieved proficiency in English beyond the use of the most basic words. But in his own homeland there was no need to explain—he could demonstrate to his friends the way he and his tribe had hunted, speared salmon, used a rope to climb up and down canyon walls, swum rapids, camped, and lived their lives while remaining concealed.

Ishi's most valuable possession in his former life had always been his bow. For the camping trip he packed a bow he had made of mountain juniper, his customary choice. For arrows he chose those made from hazel branches. To hold his bow and arrows, he preferred a quiver made from a mountain lion tail. But for the camping trip he chose his old quiver of otter skin. It had been pilfered by members of the survey party but had been donated by them to the university's museum after Ishi's arrival, along with other plundered items.

Ishi's archery technique was unlike ours. He shot his arrows either kneeling or crouching down on his haunches to avoid being seen by his prey, rather than from the standing position that we assume. He held his bow at an angle or horizontally to maintain his cover.

He always endeavored to shoot from close enough to ensure the best chance of success, and his arrows were feathered for accuracy rather than distance. He did not strive for the spectacular.

Often, he would call his game in. He could call in jackrabbits, wildcats, coyotes, deer, and sometimes even bears. He could imitate the squirrel's chatter, the goose's honk, and the voices of several birds and other animals. Once Pope tested him by having him make twelve calls to see how many animals would respond. Ishi called in five rabbits and a bobcat.

Generally, Ishi shot his prey within a range of ten to twenty yards, but sometimes he shot rabbits approaching his call from as close as five yards. He was also accurate at greater distance. Pope reported seeing Ishi shoot an arrow through a squirrel's head at forty yards.

Ishi hunted deer with a deer head covering his face, sometimes moving his head to imitate a deer's movements. He would also simulate the whimper of a fawn by sucking on a folded madrone leaf between his lips.

He would wait patiently—all day if necessary—to get his deer. He shunned stalking or chasing game unless the animal was wounded.

Ishi had an easy temperament and was always genial. His friends never saw him become angry or lose his temper. He liked to joke and tease and enjoyed the times it was returned. During the camping trip he seemed particularly relaxed.

On the trip Ishi went barefoot and wore only a breechcloth, just as he had in his former life. He took his companions throughout the Yahi territory on Mill and Deer Creeks, pointing out and telling them his tribe's names for some two hundred locations, including camps and caves where members of the Yahi tribe had lived. He also named for them more than two hundred plants that the Yahi had valued for food, medicine, and other uses.

He showed them some of his favorite places, such as where he had shot an arrow into a black bear from close range and finished it off with his obsidian knife. He confirmed the location by digging up a bear paw that he had buried there many years before.

His guests were particularly interested in the camp above Deer Creek where Ishi and his family had lived undetected for several years until the survey party stumbled upon it. The camp had originally held five of them: Ishi, his mother, his sister, and an old man and a younger one who were distantly related or unrelated to Ishi's family. The younger man died early on, leaving the remaining four of them to go it alone.

The camp was located in a steep canyon on a narrow ledge some five hundred feet above the south side of Deer Creek, close to where Sulphur Creek merged into it. Trees growing on the ledge obscured any view of the camp from the creek below or from the other side of the canyon. The cliff behind the camp rose above it two hundred feet, and its overhanging ledge protected the camp from discovery or attack from above. Forbidding thickets of chaparral surrounded the camp.

A grizzly bear had previously made his den at the camp location, and in their own language the Yahi called the camp the Grizzly Bear's Hiding Place. The Yahi used the faint trails left by the grizzly to and from the camp, avoiding overuse to keep their existence hidden.

In the camp the Yahi lived in an A-shaped main house about four feet high and tightly constructed of branches and bark. Their fire pit and cooking area were covered with a low brush roof for protection from the weather and to diffuse the smoke. Ishi's work area, where he made bows and arrows and chipped obsidian for his arrow points and knives, was located a short distance away.

They drank from a hollowed-out, shaded reservoir about three feet deep and slightly larger in diameter. They packed it with snow and drank the melt while it lasted to save themselves a trip to the creek five hundred feet below.

During the summer months, Ishi and his family, like their ancestors, made the four-day journey to Mt. Lassen to escape the heat of the foothills and to camp, hunt, and play.

When Ishi's camping trip with his San Francisco friends had run its course, he was the first to begin taking down their tents and loading up the pack animals. At the train station he responded amiably to the friendly crowd, but when the train arrived, he was the first to board it.

Ishi and his three friends vowed to return to the Lassen foothills in the autumn and again the next year, but they never did. World War I intervened, and the following year Ishi contracted tuberculosis. He departed this world on March 25, 1916, unafraid to cross into the unknown.

ISHI'S LEGACY

ISHI'S STORY IS BOTH poignant and uplifting. Throughout he showed extraordinary courage, an indomitable spirit, and an admirable adaptability. His devastating life experiences would have destroyed most people, but he took events as they occurred and made the best of them. He fully expected to meet his death outside Oroville, but life surprised him. He grabbed the opportunity and flourished during his time in civilization.

Early on and again later in his new life, Ishi was given the choice to return as a free man to his homeland, to go to an Indian reservation, or to remain living in his apartment in the museum building. He was emphatic in his choice to remain in his apartment surrounded by people he knew.

For four years Ishi presented his friends with a small window into his former world, particularly on the camping trip to his homeland. During it he showed an intimate knowledge of the land, its wildlife, and its plants that is beyond our ken. We can study nature with our intellect, scientific aids, and data and know much about it. But we are studying it from the outside. Ishi and his tribe were on the inside; to them nature was life itself.

The Yahi culture is lost to us, but Ishi's story is not. His ability to rise above the loss of his people, the loss of his culture, and the loss of all who spoke his language is truly inspirational. He leaped a huge chasm between two unrelated realms. The key to his survival in both was his adaptability. In our ever-changing present world, it would benefit us to make that aspect of Ishi's life part of our own.

Saving the Condor

SAVING THE CONDOR

I N 1987 THE ENDANGERED last wild California condor soared through the skies. He caught the updrafts effortlessly with his ten-foot wingspan and glided for miles without flapping his wings. In the right conditions he could travel more than a hundred miles in two hours. For months the condor recovery team had been trying without success to trap him.

The last wild condor had been just a furry chick in 1980 when the newly formed condor recovery team had first trapped him to take his measurements and a blood sample. Four years later they had trapped him again to attach radio transmitters to his wings, and he became known as "AC9," Adult Condor 9.

By 1985, only he and eight other condors existed in the wild. The recovery team trapped three of them that year for shipment to the San Diego and Los Angeles zoos, which were important participants in the recovery effort.

The next year, AC9 mated with AC8, the last free female condor. She produced an egg that failed and later a second that was retrieved by the recovery team and sent to the San Diego Zoo to hatch. On the same day her egg hatched at the zoo, AC8 was captured, leaving only male condors in the wild.

By 1987 just two were traversing the skies. In February, the recovery team trapped one, while AC9 peered down from a nearby oak tree and watched the capture. He was now alone, the last free condor.

THE CALIFORNIA CONDOR

UP UNTIL THEN, CALIFORNIA condors had soared the skies for more than forty thousand years. They had devoured the flesh of dead mammoths and shared in saber-tooth tigers' kills. The question now was whether the California condor would join the mammoth and the saber-tooth tiger in the dark void with no end.

The California condor has a ten-foot wingspan, the largest of any bird in North America. Its body and wings are black with a sizable triangular white patch on the underside of the adult's wings. Condors glide with their wings positioned straight out and stable, unlike the smaller common turkey vulture, which holds its wings in a slight V and often rocks while gliding.

Condors do not inflict death; they search and find it. They feed solely on carrion, usually that of large animals. They recycle death into life.

Long ago the California condor occupied much of North America. With the advancing settlement of the American West, condors retreated to California and relative safety. The California gold rush brought that safety to an end, and the condor population began to plummet toward the black hole of extinction.

Extinction was largely ignored back then. The country's bison, which had numbered in the tens of millions and occupied huge swaths of landscape, were slaughtered to a population of a few hundred that could be enclosed in a pasture.

The passenger pigeon was once the country's most abundant bird, flying in massive flocks that darkened the skies for hours on end. They were killed so wantonly that the last one, named Martha, died at the Cincinnati Zoo in 1914.

Thousands of species of animals, insects, and plants have been obliterated from the land of the living by the forces of extinction, generally without our noticing or caring. But the condor is so big that we did notice, and it became symbolic.

Condors are smart birds. They need patience and mental acuity to negotiate the shifting truces and treaties with the other animals feeding at death sites, where a single miscalculation can be fatal. Unfortunately, their intelligence does not protect them from humans. Ironically, it is only humans that can save them.

THE CAPTURE OF AC9

BY 1987 THE RECOVERY program was still trying to capture AC9. They could track him by the signals from his radio transmitter, but they could not catch him.

The man charged with the task was Peter Bloom. He had trapped thousands of birds and was the condor trapper for the recovery program. He had watched as AC9 scrutinized his capture of other condors. Bloom suspected that AC9 was employing the knowledge he had gained from those captures to avoid his own.

On an April evening in 1987, Bloom received a call that AC9 had landed on a branch near one of the traps he had placed in the Bitter Creek National Wildlife Refuge in Kern County. Bloom called his team that night, and they assembled in the dark the next morning, Easter Sunday.

They finished their preparations in the black of night so everything was ready by the first light of dawn. Bloom had modified his traps somewhat and avoided test-firing the capture net, as he usually did, so as not to alert the wary AC9. When all was ready, Bloom hid several feet away from the calf carcass being used as bait.

Condors enjoy their sleep and are not early birds. At mid-morning AC9 flew down from his perch and landed several yards away from the calf carcass. He watched warily as some ravens picked at it. A few minutes later he moved up to the carcass and lowered his head to feed.

Bloom fired the net over him and raced to the trapped condor. He and his team disentangled AC9 from the net, placed him in a carrier called a sky kennel, and drove him to the Oxnard Airport for transport to the San Diego Zoo.

For Bloom the capture of AC9 was bittersweet. He felt pride in a job well done but only sadness at the necessity of having to remove the last condor from the wild in the desperate effort to save the species from extinction.

For AC9 the experience was both terrifying and infuriating. His home of thousands of square miles had shrunk to a quarantine pen the size of a large room. Fully extended, his wings spread across half of the pen. Through its mesh top he could see the clouds, but he could not glide among them. AC9 showed his displeasure by puffing out the air sacs near his neck as his head and neck turned a furious red.

Once cleared from quarantine, he was transferred to a somewhat larger pen, but he was still confined. He was alive, but whether he would ever again float the rivers of air above California was unclear.

THE RECOVERY PROGRAM

PREVIOUS EFFORTS TO RESCUE the California condor had suffered from a lack of knowledge of the reasons the condor was diving toward extinction. In 1979 the U.S. Fish and Wildlife Service and the National Audubon Society established a recovery program to make a final concerted effort to save it.

The Fish and Wildlife Service appointed one of its own biologists, Noel Snyder, as its field representative. Snyder had no experience with condors but had previously worked to save two other endangered bird species. He proved to be a particularly wise choice.

Snyder had no preconceptions as to the cause of the steep decline in the condor population, but almost everybody else did, and they were generally wrong. As Snyder said, "We needed information. Everybody had a theory then, but nobody had the database to support their point of view."

Snyder and the Audubon Society's representative decided to begin their efforts in the spring of 1980 with what they thought were small, safe steps. They planned to enter two condor cave nests, each containing a chick, and take blood samples and measurements while a cameraman filmed the operation.

For the first attempt the team went to the top of a cliff, some eighty feet above the cave containing the nest. As they picked their way down, the two condor parents flew off leaving the chick alone.

The team gathered up the chick, later known as AC9, weighed him and took several measurements. While the team took a blood sample,

Snyder collected some eggshell fragments and condor feathers from the cave in the hope that they might shed light on the cause of the excessive condor deaths. The whole process took about ten minutes.

The next day they went to a second cliff site, which involved a steeper more treacherous climb down. They left that task to young biologist Bill Lehman and the cameraman, both professional climbers. Lehman dropped into the cave first, followed by the cameraman.

The chick put up a fight and Lehman had trouble calming it enough to take measurements. At one point during the struggle, the bird began to act strangely, then suddenly became listless and fell dead. Its demise was later determined to have been caused by stress.

Snyder knew the political repercussions for the program would be very serious, but he did not flinch.

He flew with the dead chick to the San Diego Zoo, observed the autopsy, and took full responsibility for the death. It was prominent news in much of the country and important enough for Walter Cronkite to mention it on his nightly television news show. David Brower, a director of Friends of the Earth and former director of the Sierra Club, denounced the rescue program as the "condor disposal program."

Critics clamored for the program's end and advocated for habitat preservation as the only way to save the condor. Snyder was confident that there was sufficient habitat for condors, and suspected another reason for their precipitous decline. He did not express his disagreement publicly, though, as he thought habitat preservation was always beneficial and generally needed—at least for other species.

The California Department of Fish and Game stopped just short of ending the program. Going forward, the team would be allowed only to observe—no handling or trapping of condors. Snyder kept his group ready and engaged by having them monitor condor activities and nest sites.

The team members observed AC9 closely and saw his halting, clumsy first attempts at flight. When some 15 ravens surrounded and threatened young AC9, the team watched as he fought back, puffing up and angling his wings high above his head to appear larger, and jabbing his sharp beak at any raven within range. The ravens finally retreated.

The following year, the rescue program members were monitoring a condor nest with an egg when they observed the egg roll out of the nest and over the edge of the cliff to destruction below. They watched as the breeding pair established another nest site. Soon they were delighted to discover that the female had laid another egg to replace the shattered one. This established that condors double clutched—in other words, a female condor who lost an egg would lay a second one to replace it.

The discovery was of immense importance, for the recovery team could now double the number of condor eggs laid each year. By removing a mother condor's first egg to hatch in captivity, they could induce her to lay a replacement egg to hatch in the wild. Of course, they would need permission to remove any eggs, and they knew that was impossible at the time.

That summer the father of one of the few condor chicks disappeared. With only one parent to tend to it, the chick's future was in jeopardy. The recovery team obtained emergency approval to trap the chick for rearing in captivity.

Snyder knew that another mistake would be the death knell of the program, so he asked his friend Phil Ensley, the San Diego Zoo's veterinarian, to help. They captured the chick without incident.

Later the same year the program obtained permission to trap an adult wild condor. Snyder brought in experienced trapper Pete Bloom. In the uneasy minutes before Bloom fired the capture net, with the program on the line, Snyder whispered to Ensley and Bloom, "It's a privilege and an honor to be here with you guys."

Bloom fired the net and captured the condor. As required under the terms of permission, the bird was tested to ascertain its sex. If determined to be female, it was to be taken to the Los Angeles Zoo to mate; if male, it was to be released into the wild after outfitted with tags and a radio transmitter.

When it tested as male, Snyder argued against releasing it. The condor was shy of breeding age by at least four years. With the high condor mortality rate in the wild, Snyder thought it far wiser to keep the bird safe in captivity so it could eventually breed.

The program administrators overrode Snyder and ordered him to release it. A year and a half later, the condor was dead. Its cause of death was determined to be lead poisoning, although some claimed it was politics.

In 1982, the recovery program made a breakthrough that allowed a precise count of condors in the wild. Snyder had asked friend and ornithologist Eric Johnson, a professor at Cal Poly in San Luis Obispo, to help photograph the birds. Johnson, in turn, had enlisted the help of his students to take the photographs.

When Johnson began to assemble and organize the resulting photos, he noticed that he could distinguish individual birds by telltale scars or wing feathers. From the photos, Snyder and Johnson were able to determine confidently that as of the summer of 1982 there were just over twenty condors existing in the wild.

The desperate state of the California condor, revealed by the photographic census, was an urgent call to action. Coupled with the evidence of mother condors' practice of double clutching, it persuaded the California Fish and Game Commission in 1983 to approve the removal of all first-laid eggs. In addition, the commission permitted the placement of radio transmitters on the remaining condors to allow tracking.

Egg removal is a delicate operation: if the incubating condor is startled, its hasty jump off the egg can cause it to roll away and break. Snyder called in Bill Toone from the San Diego Zoo to aid in the first retrieval.

The egg removal went off without a hitch, and the following successful hatching of the condor chick in captivity received national publicity. The next spring, the recovery program successfully removed three more eggs and hatched the chicks. Optimism reigned—often a worrisome portent.

A BAD YEAR

NOEL SNYDER REMEMBERS 1985 as the worst year of his professional life. One condor from each of three of the four wild breeding pairs died, leaving only one wild breeding pair intact. That pair lost its first egg to a bacterial infection, but the female did lay a second. Then the male of the fourth breeding pair died in August of 1985.

In total six wild condors died that year, leaving only nine remaining outside captivity. Snyder and his team pointed to the 40 percent death rate for wild condors in the year as a compelling reason to bring in the few remaining.

They also pointed to recently acquired genetic knowledge that indicated that the captive flock represented a limited number of condor families and did not contain enough genetic diversity to assure the long-term survival of the species. The unanimous opinion of expert geneticists was that the wild condors should be added to the existing captive flock to assure sufficient genetic diversity for breeding purposes.

The U.S. Fish and Wildlife Service had prohibited condor trapping, primarily due to the Audubon Society's stand against it—that is, until the last male of the four wild breeding pairs died. At that point the Fish and Wildlife Service relented and approved an emergency plan to trap the remaining wild condors.

Surprisingly, the Audubon Society filed suit to block any trapping of wild condors and obtained a court injunction to prevent it.

Long a primary force in efforts to save the condor—the organization opposed capture for reasons that were never clear. But they appeared to be related to its campaign to acquire a huge tract of land for condor habitat. It feared that the capture of all wild condors would undercut that campaign—and perhaps also future habitat-acquisition campaigns. The Audubon Society was unwilling to admit in the face of mounting evidence that wild condors were dying primarily from lead poisoning acquired from eating bullet fragments in carcasses of wildlife that had been shot.

The Audubon Society's stand and the injunction produced greater harm when one of the remaining wild condors was trapped and determined to have a dangerous level of lead poisoning. Snyder argued that the lead-poisoned condor could be cured in captivity but was almost sure to die if released.

But the Audubon Society refused to back off its position and, using the injunction, compelled the release of the condor back into the wild. It soon died, just as Snyder had predicted, and the details of its forced release and death became public.

On appeal, several important conservation groups joined the U.S. Fish and Wildlife Service in filing briefs in opposition to the injunction. They argued that the continued survival of the California condor was at stake—that trapping the remaining condors was the only possible way to avoid extinction.

In 1986 the appellate court reversed the injunction and permitted the trapping. Eventually the Audubon Society corrected its destructive course and again became a staunch supporter of the condors' rescue. It also acquired the large tract that it had feared losing.

Once the approval to trap the remaining wild condors was secure, Snyder resigned from the recovery program having accomplished his goals for it. But two large obstacles remained: the successful breeding of condors in captivity and the release of captive-bred condors able to survive successfully in the wild.

The breeding of captive condors proved relatively easy, aided by the scientific advances in genetics. Previously, the program would have bred AC9 with his former mate, AC8. However, by the time of AC9's capture in 1987, the close family connection between them was known, and AC8 was paired with an unrelated condor.

The next spring, she hatched a healthy chick, the first bred in captivity. The recovery program hatched more chicks, and by the summer of 1991 the captive condor population was up to fifty. The time was coming to release some.

In January 1992, Noel Snyder and many other participants gathered to watch the first release of captive-raised California condors into the wild. After a gloomy five years when California condors existed only in cages, there was good reason to celebrate their return to the skies.

The releases met with mixed success. The released condors, all bred in captivity, were overly friendly with people and occasionally flew into power lines and were electrocuted. Fortunately, the program was able to mitigate most of those problems with aversive conditioning.

However, the primary cause of condor deaths, lead poisoning from bullet fragments in wildlife carcasses, remained stubbornly insoluble.

The condor's range was great, and banning hunters from using lead bullets over such an expansive area was not yet politically feasible. Still, the captive breeding program had been successful enough to continue the release of condors.

AC8'S RELEASE

In 2000, AC8, THE last wild female condor captured, became the first wild condor to be freed. She had spent fourteen years at the San Diego Zoo and produced twenty eggs during that time but was no longer fertile.

Back in the wild, she ranged far and wide over the California terrain, much farther than the captive-raised birds. In November 2002 she was picked up with acute lead poisoning. Cured through extraordinary medical efforts, she was released into the wild again. She soon returned to the Tejon Ranch, a traditional home area for her.

In early 2003 Britton Cole Lewis and his father, both experienced hunters, drove into the Tejon Ranch for a weekend of hunting. The ranch charged $20,000 to hunt elk, $4000 to hunt bear, and $400 to hunt boar, the Lewises' quarry.

After Britton and his father had hunted unsuccessfully for some time, Britton raised his rifle at a large bird perched high in a tree. With his scope trained on the bird, it is likely that he saw the prominent number tags on the bird's wings. He squeezed the trigger, and AC8 fell from her perch into a motionless crumple splayed across an upper branch. As later revealed, Britton's father looked up at the bird and said:

"Goddamn, Brit. I think you shot a fucking condor."

Mark Hall, the manager of the Hopper Mountain National Wildlife Refuge, noticed during the weekend that AC8's transmitter was showing no movement. He was virtually certain something bad had happened to her, but he was unable to check on her until Tuesday.

Hall arranged for a hunting guide to help him locate the bird in the ranch's remote mountains. After riding a while, they arrived at an oak tree where the dark mass of AC8 hung high in its branches.

Hall climbed up the tree and shook AC8 loose. She had been shot through her chest. He examined the surrounding area but saw no vehicle tracks, no footprints, no shell casings—no evidence at all.

He preserved AC8's body in an ice chest and drove back. The recovery team was grief stricken. Their work over the years and AC8's heroics had been extinguished by a hunter's heedless stupidity.

U.S. Fish and Wildlife special agent Brett Dickerson was determined to catch the culprit. The Tejon Ranch records disclosed that only a dozen individuals had paid to hunt that particular weekend. The special agents interviewed all twelve of the hunters, and one mentioned that he had seen a father and son shooting at birds.

The agents separated Britton Lewis and his father and interviewed them at the same time. Each denied knowing about the shooting of a condor, but when Dickerson told the father that a hunter had reported they were shooting at birds, the father's response aroused his suspicions. The father replied that the other hunter might have assumed so because his son had been sighting on a few crows.

During his interview of the father, Dickerson received a call from the agent interviewing the son. The father misinterpreted Dickerson's responses to indicate that his son had confessed, and so he related to Dickerson the details of his son's killing of the condor. When confronted with his father's account, Britton Lewis confessed to shooting the condor but insisted that he had thought it was a turkey vulture.

Condors were and are protected federally under the Endangered Species Act. As interpreted by the courts, the Act required the prosecution to prove beyond a reasonable doubt that the defendant *knew* he was shooting a condor.

The prosecution did not believe it could prove that, but it did force Lewis to plead guilty to a less serious offense under the Migratory Bird Treaty Act and to the unrelated offense of poaching a deer and transporting it across state lines. Lewis was sentenced to five years of probation, a ban on any hunting during that time, forfeiture of his rifle, a large fine, and two hundred hours of community service.

AC9 RETURNS TO THE WILD

FOR YEARS AC9 HAD been the favorite among members of the recovery program. He had been the first chick they trapped and tagged. He had fathered the last condor egg then laid in the wild. And through his elusive ways, he had evaded capture long enough to become the last condor taken from the wild. He fathered fifteen chicks while in captivity.

The recovery program decided to free AC9 in 2002. Before his release, they moved him to a holding pen in a remote area of harsh country looking out on cliffs, caves, and chaparral.

AC8 saw her old mate from the air and landed on the pen. She tore at its wire mesh in a futile attempt to reach AC9. Frustrated in her efforts, she reluctantly gave up and flew away.

In May of 2002 they finally released AC9 back into the wild. He had been confined for fifteen years, but now he was liberated—to glide and ride the updrafts—to fly free in a sky of condors. The recovery program had at last come full circle.

In 2016, fourteen years after his return to the skies, AC9 left the cave where he and his mate were caring for their three-month-old chick. His transmitter failed a short time later. AC9 has not been seen since and is presumed dead.

THE RECOVERY

To RESTORE AN ENDANGERED species on a long-term basis it is necessary to remedy the essential reason for its decline. In the condor's case the remedy required was a prohibition on the use of lead bullets by hunters.

In 2008 the California legislature finally reacted to widespread support for the condor's recovery and banned the use of lead bullets for hunting large animals in the condor's range in Central and Southern California. Since 2019, hunting with lead bullets has been prohibited throughout the state.

The condor recovery program has been a huge success. As of this writing there are more that five hundred California condors in the world, and over three hundred flying wild. Most of them are soaring the skies over California from Big Sur and Pinnacles National Park to Southern California. But the release area has been expanded beyond the state, and California condors are now flying the skies over northern Arizona, southern Utah, and Mexico's Baja.

In March of 2021 the U.S. Fish and Wildlife Service announced plans to release California condors in far Northern California, Oregon, and northwestern Nevada. It intends to release some into California's Redwood National Park, where they have been absent from their perches on old growth redwoods for more than a hundred years.

Imagine seeing a California condor gliding the updrafts, its huge black wings silhouetted against a blue sky, as it floats in to land on a high branch of an old forest redwood. The sight would be thrilling.

The condor's decline and recovery are a measure both of our destructive impact and our ability, when focused, to remedy our actions. The California condor is a success story. We can all celebrate and hail the condor. But it took the better part of a half century, against seemingly impossible odds and various political pressures to preserve the condor. We have to act earlier. We have to do better.

Consider the choices: Preservation is faith in the future. Extinction looks backward to loss. Preservation is a birth of hope. Extinction is its death. Preservation is possibilities. Extinction is oblivion. We need to choose preservation—for the future of our children, for the future of our children's children and for the future of our fellow animal, bird, and insect residents living on this glorious planet.

The True Prize

THE TRUE PRIZE

O**FTEN IN LIFE, ONE** random step leads to another, and only in looking back is a path discernible. For John Steinbeck that step occurred in the late summer of 1936 when he wrote a series of articles about California's Dust Bowl migrants for the *San Francisco News.*

The step seemed no different from those Steinbeck had taken before. But it was. It led to the peak years of his writing, perhaps of his life, and to recognition and fame. It was the time of his making, and for a period afterwards, his undoing.

Steinbeck's own vulnerability showed through during those years, revealing his raw inner emotions and, in essence, his soul.

Steinbeck was a loner in his youth. Born in Salinas in 1902 and raised there, he did not share the conservative temper of the Central California agricultural town. Never a joiner, Steinbeck was socially inept and perceived as an outsider by his classmates and neighbors. For his part he felt rejected by them. Socially isolated, he spent half of his youth immersed in dreams and fantasies.

During his freshman year of high school, he decided to be a writer, and he never wavered from that choice. He spent six sporadic years at Stanford University without ever coming close to earning a degree, attending some literature and writing courses and assembling a host of incompletes in other subjects.

Then and afterward, he worked a variety of temporary jobs. He worked as a surveyor above the Big Sur coastline, as a ranch hand near King City, and as a laborer with a dredging crew draining a swamp. He broke horses for army officers, was a caretaker in Tahoe, and worked several stints for Spreckels Sugar Company, generally at night.

In 1930 he married Carol Henning, an intelligent and independent woman with a keen sense of humor. Steinbeck bestowed his highest praise on her in writing to a friend, "Horses like her and dogs and little boys and boot blacks and laborers."

For a time, they lived rent free in a three-room cottage owned by Steinbeck's father in Pacific Grove near the ocean. It was the Depression, but generally a happy time for Steinbeck. They had a wide group of friends without money like them. Steinbeck later wrote, "We pooled our troubles, our money when we had some, our inventiveness, and our pleasure." He was committed to writing and declared, "Nothing will ever stop me!"

His father encouraged his desire to be a writer, but his mother disapproved and wanted him to be something more respectable, such as a banker. Steinbeck later wrote of his father's support, "He admired anyone who laid down his line and followed it undeflected to the end. . . . He was a man intensely disappointed in himself. And I think he liked the complete ruthlessness of my design to be a writer in spite of my mother and hell."

STEINBECK AMONG THE MIGRANTS

THE DUST BOWL OF the 1930s encompassed the panhandles of Oklahoma and Texas and portions of several neighboring states. There the wind blew the desiccated and depleted topsoil off the land, creating masses of dust that blotted out the sun and coated the withered crops. The banks and corporations followed the dust and scooped up the small farms—foreclosing on them or purchasing them on the cheap—and evicted the farmers from their homes.

Employing tractors instead of human hands, the new owners displaced the farm workers from their jobs. Finally, poverty chased the people from their Dust Bowl communities and herded them onto roads toward California. Lured by handbills advertising for farm work and by their dreams of a better life, the migrants left their homes with nothing but their beat-up vehicles, their meager belongings, and hope.

The migrants thought of California as a sugar bowl, with its ripe fruit hanging heavy on the trees and its vegetable produce flourishing out of the fertile earth. But the reality they discovered was starkly different.

In 1936 the *San Francisco News* asked Steinbeck to observe the migrant reality and to write several articles for the *News* about it. California's governmental authorities had largely ignored the migrants' crushing poverty and hunger, and the public was generally unaware of it. Only the federal Resettlement Administration was attempting to alleviate the migrants' terrible living conditions by establishing some sanitary camps for them.

Steinbeck talked to Resettlement Administration officials about the migrants and bought an old bakery truck so as to better fit in with them. He drove down through the Central Valley, stopping at a number of squatters' camps and farm labor camps. Steinbeck had previously seen and experienced hobo groups, labor camps, and migrant slums near Salinas. But the desperate, beaten-down inhabitants he saw living in starvation conditions shocked and infuriated him.

Steinbeck met Tom Collins on a rainy September evening at the Resettlement Administration's Arvin Sanitary Camp for migrants known as "Weedpatch," located about twenty miles south of Bakersfield. When Steinbeck arrived, the sodden migrants were crowded around a table and looking patiently at Collins, a slight man in a frayed suit.

Collins was in charge of the camp, deeply committed to the migrants, and trying to halt the disease then running rampant among the camp's inhabitants. The migrants had measles, mumps, whooping cough, and other illnesses and Collins was trying to help them in any way he could. Upon meeting Steinbeck, Collins took him to his own shack for a quick cup of coffee, but before they could talk, there was a riot in the sewing room then serving as a quarantine area for children with measles.

Fights were breaking out and children were wailing, Steinbeck recalled, "and Tom Collins trotted back and forth explaining, coaxing, now and then threatening, trying to keep peace in the miserable wet slum until daylight should come." Steinbeck described Collins as having large, dark eyes that were "tired beyond sleepiness, the kind of tired that won't let you sleep even if you have time and a bed."

Steinbeck spent several days with Collins and through him was able to talk to the migrants and view their lives up close. Collins also provided Steinbeck with the lengthy reports he had written to his superiors, containing the details of migrant life and capturing their conversational language.

Upon passing through Salinas, Steinbeck saw his home town consumed by a vigilante war against the striking migrant workers protesting their meager pay and the harsh working conditions in the lettuce fields. Clerks, salesmen, and other ordinary locals had become vigilantes bearing axes and other weapons, determined to beat and intimidate the "red" strikers.

The strikers' civil rights were ignored completely and some were rounded up and held in an internment camp. No city, county, or state authorities attempted to suppress or even tamp down the violence committed by the vigilantes. Steinbeck saw it as the ugly face of fascism on the march, and he took it personally.

At the end of September, Steinbeck traveled to Weedpatch again, spending days with Collins as his guide. Upon his return he wrote to his literary agents, "I just returned yesterday from the strike area of Salinas and from my migrants in Bakersfield. This thing is dangerous."

Steinbeck thought the *San Francisco News* would be intimidated by the powerful forces oppressing the migrants and that his articles would never see the light of day. He wrote to a friend that "the labor situation is so tense just now that the *News* is scared and won't print the series. Any reference to labor except as dirty dogs is not printed by the big press out here."

But the *News* held firm and published Steinbeck's seven articles in consecutive daily installments in early October of 1936. Steinbeck's first article angrily and bluntly assessed the situation of California's more than 150,000 homeless migrants:

> At the season of the year, when California's great crops are coming into harvest, the heavy grapes, the prunes, the apples and lettuce and the rapidly maturing cotton, our highways swarm with the migrant workers, that shifting group of nomadic, poverty-stricken harvesters driven by hunger and the threat of hunger from crop to crop, from harvest to harvest ... And so they move, frantically, with starvation close behind them.

His second article focused more on individuals: "Here, in the faces of the husband and his wife, you begin to see an expression you will notice on every face; not worry, but absolute terror of the starvation that crowds in against the borders of the camp." He was particularly disturbed by the number of children listless from malnutrition or actually starving to death.

Steinbeck felt great compassion for the migrants, but his anger at their situation overwhelmed him and poisoned his writing. He had started and thrown away one book about them, and was now struggling with a new novel, one still tainted by his excessive anger.

THE TURNING POINT

THE TURNING POINT FOR Steinbeck as a writer occurred during February and March of 1938 when he joined Collins amid devastating floods that were causing widespread starvation in the migrant camps in Visalia and Nipomo. He wrote his literary agent, Elizabeth Otis, in February of 1938, just before leaving for the camps: "There are about five thousand families starving to death over there, not just hungry but actually starving."

When he met Collins at the flooded camps, the situation was beyond dire. As Collins described it: "For forty-eight hours, and without food or sleep, we worked among the sick and half-starved people, dragging some from under trees to a different sort of shelter, dragging others from torn and ragged tents, floored with inches of water, stagnant water."

Steinbeck and Collins finally collapsed and slept in the mud. When Collins woke, he "found John lying on his back. He was a mass of mud and slime. His face was a mucky mask punctuated with eyes, a nose, and mouth."

After two weeks in the fields, Steinbeck went home to Los Gatos for a brief respite, returning two days later for another week of work in the flooded fields. The starvation of the children there gnawed at his insides.

During the floods, Steinbeck and the migrants worked together to rescue the helpless. He and the migrants suffered the same wet, the same cold, and the same lack of almost everything else. Laboring in the emergency conditions side by side, they developed a closeness. Steinbeck became one of them—no longer an outsider—and they became a part of him.

Soon afterward he wrote an article arising out of the experience called "Starvation Under the Orange Trees," but no one would publish it. Finally, his local paper, the small *Monterey Trader*, printed it in April of 1938.

Until then Steinbeck had been hard at work on a novel attacking the vigilantes and others who oppressed the migrants, but in May he abandoned and destroyed the novel without ever sending it out. He explained his reason in a letter to Elizabeth Otis: "It is bad because it is not honest. . . . My whole work drive has been aimed at making people understand each other and then I deliberately write this book the aim of which is to cause hatred through partial understanding."

Within days of junking it, he began writing *The Grapes of Wrath*. The books he had destroyed had taken up two years of his time, but he had finally written the poison out of his system. He was thirty-six years old.

Steinbeck wrote *The Grapes of Wrath* in one sustained, inspired stretch between June and October of 1938. It was revolutionary in its advocacy and compassion for the migrants, at a time when few noticed or spoke out for them. It narrated the migration of the fictional Joad family from the Oklahoma Dust Bowl to California and portrayed their often brutal experiences in the state. Steinbeck wanted the book to be personal rather than ideological, to pierce people and to grip their emotions.

In the journal he kept while writing the novel, Steinbeck counseled himself:

"Begin the detailed description of the family I am to live with for four months. Must take time in the description, detail, detail, looks, clothes, gestures. . . . We have to know these people." On another day he reminded himself: "Make the people live. Make them live."

Steinbeck had already achieved some success with *Tortilla Flat* and great success with *Of Mice and Men*, but he knew his new book was something bigger, that it occupied a higher plane. He confided to himself in his journal, "For the first time I am working on a real book that is not limited and that will take every bit of experience and thought and feeling that I have."

A week later, he noted in his journal again, "If only I could do this book properly it would be one of the really fine books and a truly American book." He then confessed to self-doubts: "But I am assailed with my own ignorance and inability. . . . For no one else knows my lack of ability the way I do."

The Grapes of Wrath is engrossing because Steinbeck portrays in story form the awful reality he saw and knew. He describes carloads of oranges and other foods destroyed to prop up prices, while the "coroners fill in the [death] certificates—died of malnutrition—because the food must rot, must be forced to rot."

He describes guards holding the starving migrants back from the food being destroyed, while "in the eyes of the hungry there is a growing wrath. In the souls of the people the grapes of wrath are filling and growing heavy, growing heavy for the vintage."

From the time Steinbeck began writing *Grapes*, he had the conclusion in his mind. The book ends with Rose of Sharon, the Joad daughter who has just lost her baby in childbirth, lying down beside a starving stranger and offering him her bare milk-filled breast.

Steinbeck's publisher pressed him to revise the final chapter. They wanted him to familiarize the reader with the stranger, to build up to the ending, and to integrate it more into the story. Steinbeck's reply reveals much about him:

> I am sorry but I cannot change that ending. It is casual—there is no fruity climax. . . . It must be a stranger, and it must be quick. . . . And if I'm wrong, I'm alone in my wrongness. . . . One other thing—I am not writing a satisfying story. I've done my damnedest to rip a reader's nerves to rags, I don't want him satisfied.
>
> And one more thing—I tried to write this book the way lives are being lived not the way books are written.

The book's conclusion remained unchanged.

Steinbeck dedicated the book to the two people most important to it. The dedication read:

To
CAROL
who willed this book.
To
TOM
who lived it.

His wife Carol had pushed and encouraged him in his writing. Carol was his chief editor, correcting and revising the book as she transformed Steinbeck's cramped handwriting into type.

Steinbeck had been searching for a title for months before Carol came up with her magical solution, *The Grapes of Wrath*, from a line in "The Battle Hymn of the Republic." Steinbeck thought the title brilliant. His book was revolutionary, and by reference to "The Battle Hymn," the title both incorporated the country's revolutionary tradition and stamped the book as undeniably American.

Tom was, of course, Tom Collins, Steinbeck's all-purpose guide to the migrant soul.

The Grapes of Wrath was published in April of 1939. Almost immediately it became the number one seller in the country, and it stayed in the top position for months. The movie rights sold quickly for $75,000, a huge sum at the time. Steinbeck made sure Collins was hired at a good salary as an advisor for the film. The next year Steinbeck won the Pulitzer Prize for *The Grapes of Wrath*.

THE AFTERMATH

STEINBECK'S COMPLETION OF THE book closed a chapter on his life. It left him totally exhausted, physically ill, and in a deep depression. An infection had spread throughout his body, and for the next year his back and a leg were so crippled that he needed help going up and down stairs and climbing in and out of a car.

His marriage to Carol was falling apart too. They separated within a few months of the book's publication, reconciled for a while, and divorced two years later.

He had always feared fame, and now that it was thrust on him, Steinbeck fell into a steep tailspin. He despised all the attention, the telephone calls, and the letters, many from cranks, haters, and those seeking money. Critics generally praised the book, but some expressed nothing but contempt for it.

The book was incendiary, and Steinbeck was falsely called a communist and worse. The FBI investigated him and maintained a large file on him. A friendly sheriff's deputy told him that he should never enter a hotel room alone to avoid being set up for a rape charge by those trying to get him.

It was the personal attacks that bothered Steinbeck most. He was maliciously called a pervert, a drunkard, a liar, and other epithets. But the one that stung Steinbeck the worst was the fabrication that the Okies hated him.

It was Eleanor Roosevelt who buttressed Steinbeck's credibility in the public's regard. After visiting the migrant camps in April, 1940, she was asked by a New York Times reporter about the accuracy of

Steinbeck's portrayal of conditions there. She answered, "I have never believed *The Grapes of Wrath* was exaggerated."

Steinbeck wrote to her appreciatively: "May I thank you for your kind words. I have been called a liar so constantly that sometimes I wonder whether I may not have dreamed the things I saw and heard in the period of my research."

Steinbeck groped for a way out of his deep depression, what he called "a nightmare all in all" and "the crash within myself." He tried to fall back on his natural curiosity, and his desire for change. On October 16, 1939 he wrote in his journal:

> It is one year less ten days that I finished the first draft of the *Grapes*.... The longest time I've been in many years without writing.... That part of life that made the *Grapes* is over.... I have to go to new sources and find new roots.

In mid-November, he made a new start. He was reading and studying marine life with his best friend, Ed Ricketts. Ricketts was a skilled biologist who owned a laboratory along the coast in the tidal area of Monterey. He supplied schools, researchers, and other buyers with a wide variety of marine life, from microorganisms to larger creatures, both living and dead.

In 1940 Steinbeck and Ricketts traveled by boat down the Pacific Coast of Mexico to study marine life, and shortly after the trip's conclusion Steinbeck began to write a narrative of the trip for a new book. Steinbeck also began taking flying lessons to gain a new perspective.

Still, his depression lingered. As he wrote to a friend in the fall of 1940: "The loneliness and discouragement are by no means a thing that has passed. In fact they seem to crowd in more than ever."

By the late spring of 1941 he was deep into writing the narrative for *Sea of Cortez: A Leisurely Journal of Travel and Research*, and Ricketts was writing the scientific appendix. The work of writing started to bring Steinbeck back from the depths. In June he wrote to Pascal Covici, his longtime friend and publisher's representative at Viking: "I am working as hard and as well I can and I don't dare do anything else. I've been pretty near to a number of edges and am not away from them yet by any means but I find safety in work and that is the only safety I do find."

Steinbeck was tired of people and their complications. It was a relief to be writing about invertebrates and other sea animals rather than humans. In *Sea of Cortez*, he explored the "relationships of animal to animal" and the concept "that man is related to the whole thing, related inextricably to all reality, known and unknowable." He was taking a large view, one that encompassed "the tide pool to the stars and then back to the tide pool again."

Steinbeck would soon move to the East Coast and live in New York City for many years before ultimately settling in Sag Harbor, on Long Island. Still, he tapped into his past and his California roots to write two of his most successful later books, *Cannery Row* and *East of Eden*.

He began traveling, often internationally, and living in a much wealthier social milieu. His writing suffered and when it did, he suffered as well. He felt he had lost his grounding. The last book he wrote, *Travels with Charley in Search for America*, was an attempt to make his way back to it and to the lives of ordinary people.

In 1962 he was awarded the Nobel Prize for literature, primarily for *The Grapes of Wrath*. The award brought congratulations and plaudits but also criticism that Steinbeck's best work was more than two decades old, and that he was no longer a force in current literature.

In a letter to Covici, Steinbeck addressed the criticism generously and wrote a sentence that captured his wider perspective on life: "What it boils down to is that everything exists, it is what you pick out of the grab bag of experience that matters."

Steinbeck's choice of the migrant experience and creation of *The Grapes of Wrath* was inspired, but it used up every "thought and feeling" that he had. Just weeks before finishing the book, he wrote to Elizabeth Otis: "And I'm desperately tired but I want to finish. And meanwhile I feel as though shrapnel were bursting about my head. I only hope the book is some good. Can't tell yet at all."

He was stretched to the outer limits of his writing ability where all was at risk. He was calling on every power he had to tell a story that he was impelled to tell. For Steinbeck, that—not the Nobel—was the true prize.

Note: The sources for all quotations in this story and its principal sources are listed in "Principal Sources" at the end of the book.

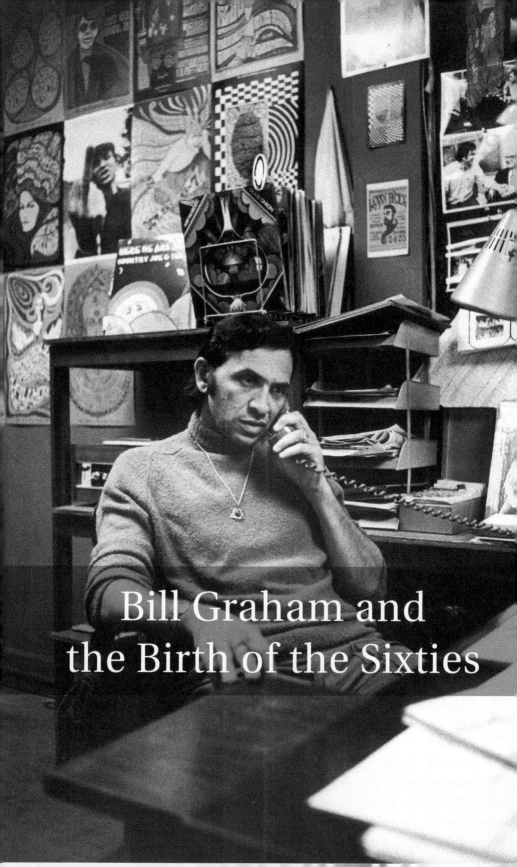

Bill Graham and
the Birth of the Sixties

BILL GRAHAM AND THE BIRTH OF THE SIXTIES

Bill Graham and rock 'n' roll—it's hard to think of one without thinking of the other, and about their impact on the sixties. The "sixties" hadn't quite arrived in 1964. Yes, maybe Mario Savio started things off with his impassioned address about free speech in December, 1964. But to my way of thinking, the real cultural change began to ride in on the beat of rock 'n' roll in 1965 and kept growing thereafter.

In 1965 the Vietnam War and the draft were expanding, spawning anti-war protests. The pill was bringing about sexual freedom. Jeans were becoming the uniform of dress, and more guys were wearing their hair long. And the music scene was changing.

It was the year Bob Dylan transformed from acoustic folk singer to electric rock prophet. He released his first album with electric songs, *Bringing It All Back Home*, in early 1965. That summer he roiled the Newport Folk Festival when he blasted out amplified electric tunes. Later, he released a fully electric album, *Highway 61 Revisited*, containing "Like a Rolling Stone" and other classics. The refrain of the album's cut of "The Ballad of a Thin Man" captured the bewilderment of the general public at the cultural change occurring before their eyes: "Something is happening here, but you don't know what it is/Do you, Mr. Jones?"

Where the tornado of change touched down early, the youth were aware of it. It carried a new freedom and a new culture, and for many it arrived on the beat of rock 'n' roll. But it was not until 1967 that the media caught on and widely recognized it. Once they did, they covered it full bore and trumpeted the "Summer of Love."

BILL

BILL GRAHAM WAS A prime catalyst and a very unlikely one. He was not a rock musician and definitely was not hip. He was born Wulf Wolodia Grajonca on January 8, 1931, in a town on the border between Germany and Poland. His father died of sepsis two days after Bill's birth, and soon afterwards his mother moved Bill and his five older sisters to Berlin.

After Kristallnacht, the Night of Broken Glass in 1938, Bill's mother became alarmed by threats to her Jewish family. She transferred Bill and his youngest sister, Tolla, to a local Jewish school to insulate them from the Hitler Youth. In 1940 the school was forced to close, and their mother sent them away to a chateau outside Paris for their schooling.

After Germany invaded France and occupied Paris in 1941, a man from the Red Cross appeared at the chateau to lead the Jewish students south. The children joined the fleeing chaos, and made the long journey on foot, tired and hungry virtually all the time and subsisting mainly on oranges.

By the time they reached Lyon, Tolla was suffering from pneumonia and malnutrition and had to be hospitalized. Bill and Tolla were close, and he wanted to stay with her, but the Red Cross man told Bill that he needed to keep moving. Tolla, he said, needed to get well and would catch up later.

From Lyon, the children walked to Marseille, took a train to Barcelona, and wound up in Madrid for several weeks during the heat of the summer. From Madrid, they made their way to Lisbon and boarded a ship, which docked at Casablanca and then Dakar before zigzagging across the Atlantic to avoid enemy ships. The children slept on deck and lived on cookies and oranges.

The boat landed in Bermuda and ultimately made port in New York on September 24, 1941. Of the sixty-five children who had begun the march from the chateau, only eleven made it to New York. Tolla was not one of them.

Bill and the other ten young refugees were bused to a Jewish placement home for foster children in Pleasantville, a couple of hours outside New York City. Its objective was to place the children as quickly as possible with foster parents willing to accept them into their homes.

Every weekend Bill, ten years old, would clean up and present himself to the visiting prospective families. And every weekend—sometimes during the week too—he was rejected. Of the eleven children who had made it to America, he was the last to be chosen. To Bill those several weeks of rejection were more painful than anything that had happened before.

On November 12, 1941, Alfred and Pearl Ehrenreich and their son Roy finally agreed to take Bill into their home in the Bronx. Bill loved his new mother, felt neutral toward his father, and considered Roy a brother and friend. Roy worked with Bill for months to help him shed his strong accent so he could fit in to American society.

After three years, Bill went looking for jobs so he could begin paying his foster family the amount they were receiving for his keep. Bill did not want somebody else paying for him. He mostly delivered groceries, working hard to please his customers and relishing their tips.

With no news from Europe of his family, Bill thought, "I'm out here on my own. I don't have anybody."

But four years after Bill's arrival in America, his sister Esther found him. Esther had been liberated by the American army from Spandau, a Nazi concentration camp. She was nineteen years old at the time and set out immediately to find her family.

She first went to Berlin where she found that the building where they had lived was totally bombed out—the entire area devastated. She knew two of her sisters had gone to Hungary so she made her way to Budapest, hiding all the way because she had no documents and no provable identity.

Esther found one sister in Budapest and learned that the other was in Vienna. She tried to make her way there but was arrested at the border by Hungarian authorities and jailed because of her lack of papers. On a work detail she escaped over the border to Austria and found her sister living in Vienna.

Esther made her way from Austria back to Germany, where she began working for the Hebrew Immigrant Aid Society. She asked her boss to help her find her brother, Bill. On his very first trip to the U.S., the boss wired her, "I found your brother."

She wrote immediately to Bill, who was elated that at least some of his family had survived. Over time, he learned that his mother been gassed at Auschwitz, that Tolla had died in France, and that his other four sisters were alive. In time Esther moved to the San Francisco Bay Area and she and Bill became close. Over the years Bill also became reacquainted with his other sisters.

As Bill grew older, he worked in the Catskills and later made an unsuccessful attempt at becoming an actor. At age 35 he launched a new career in San Francisco as a promoter of music events.

THE BEGINNING

IN NOVEMBER OF 1965 Bill put on his first rock concert, as the business manager of the San Francisco Mime Troupe. Bill had instigated arrangements for the Troupe's arrest for obscenity during one of their improvised political satire performances at a city park. He had calculated correctly that the arrest would raise the Troupe's public profile, and afterward, to raise funds for their defense, he promoted a benefit party that was successful beyond all expectations.

Thousands clogged the street and sidewalk outside the Troupe's San Francisco loft to get into the party and dance to the music of the Jefferson Airplane (before Grace Slick), the Fugs, Sandy Bull, and others.

Generally ignoring the good times inside, Bill Graham was intent upon collecting the small admission charge and posting signs like "No Inzy-Outzy" on the door. The party pulsed on until six in the morning when Allen Ginsberg brought it to a close by chanting a mantra.

Everybody else viewed the party through conventional eyes and saw it as a great time, but Bill recognized that something new was happening. He later called it "the most exciting experience of my life."

Bill later promoted a second benefit event for the Troupe, this one at the larger Fillmore Auditorium at Geary and Fillmore Streets. He headlined the Great Society with Grace Slick as lead singer and again the Jefferson Airplane, and added strobe lights that flashed on the dancers. He also raised the admissions fee from $1.00 to $1.50, but that had no effect upon the huge crowd attending.

Ralph Gleason wrote of the event in his widely followed music column in the *San Francisco Chronicle*: "Inside a most remarkable assemblage of humanity was leaping, jumping, dancing, frigging, fragging, and fruggling on the dance floor to the music of the half-dozen rock bands." Black strobe lights were pulsing, and the audience was dancing in flowing fantasy costumes, granny dresses, Goodwill cast offs, or blue jeans.

Bill Graham urged the Mime Troupe to throw more of these profit-able music events, but they said they were interested in making polit-ical statements, not money. Bill replied that people wanted a new cul-ture—that he could change more with his dance events than they ever could with their political activism. They rejected his advice and told him to do as he wished.

He would, and rock and the youth culture would never be the same.

Bill promoted his third and last benefit for the Mime Troupe in Jan-uary of 1966. The Grateful Dead, formerly known as the Warlocks, were at the bottom of the billing. It was their first time playing as the Grateful Dead and according to Jerry Garcia, it was the start of everything.

Later that month Ken Kesey and his Merry Pranksters put on the Trips Festival at the Longshoreman's Hall in San Francisco and asked Bill to provide some oversight. During the event, Bill ran around with a clipboard, while almost everyone else was literally out of their minds, some intentionally and some unsuspectingly, as the drinks were spiked with LSD. Bill was completely sober and trying to bring some order to the event. Most people there viewed him as though he were from a different planet.

A WISP OF PURITY

IN EARLY FEBRUARY OF 1966, Bill threw dance concerts at the Fillmore Auditorium on three successive nights under his soon-to-be famous trademark, "Bill Graham Presents." Giddy with the great success of those concerts, he persuaded the owner of the Fillmore to grant him a lease for his events.

He threw himself into his new profession with intensity, learning about the music scene, of which he knew little, and concentrating on pleasing his customers. He was totally consumed with his work. Artists created posters for the shows, and often Bill himself taped them up around town.

That summer, while Bill was solidifying his hold on presenting music events, Janis Joplin was emerging as the new lead singer of Big Brother and the Holding Company.

Later in the summer Grace Slick left the band headed by her then husband Darby Slick, and with his blessing became the new lead singer of the Jefferson Airplane. She brought with her two songs that would propel her and the Jefferson Airplane to fame, "Somebody to Love," written by Darby, and her own "White Rabbit."

For her song Grace used images from *Alice in Wonderland* for lyrics and set the song's hallucinatory tone with its opening: "One pill makes you larger/And one pill makes you small." It was one of the first famous psychedelic songs.

Bill's initial Fillmore events were low-key with admission easy and inexpensive. Upon handing over a ticket, you would take the offered free apple, or not, and enter the auditorium for the casual dance party. The bands were there to supply the music, and most people were dancing rather than focusing on the performers.

Many dancers wore free-flowing costumes that looked magical under the flashing strobe lights. There was a feeling of lightness and a wisp of purity, a dance to the beat of new experience without the fingerprints of image or money.

Over the next several months the dance party atmosphere changed almost imperceptibly to that of a music concert. It became more crowded, and although there was still dancing, the music became the focus. Many people simply sat on the floor and listened. As Jerry Garcia recalled, "It just sort of evolved into the rock 'n' roll palace . . . when Bill Graham took over the idea."

Bill certainly wanted to make money, but above all he loved putting on the shows. He was not young and he was not hip—he was just Bill. He was throwing a party, and although it seemed free-form, Bill made sure that the facility was prepared in all details to make the audience comfortable. After his chaotic early years, it is easy to see why he insisted upon structure and order for the events he presented.

According to Pete Townshend of the Who, Bill's focus was, "Here's the audience. Give 'em a show. Give 'em a hell of a show." Bill had merged his artistic desires with his business bent to create an entertainment enterprise that was devoted to serving its customers well. He changed the face of rock from small clubs to a spacious, comfortable venue, and the Fillmore Auditorium was the place where it happened.

In January of 1967, the Jefferson Airplane released its *Surrealistic Pillow* album, and it became a worldwide hit. In May, Scott McKenzie filled the airwaves with his song's call: "If you're going to San Francisco / Be sure to wear some flowers in your hair."

Eventually the media caught on that something was happening and pronounced the coming season the "Summer of Love." And everyone wanted a piece of it.

GOOD TIMES

THE FIRST LARGE SCALE outdoor rock festival took place on Mount Tamalpais on June 10 and 11 of 1967. It featured, among others: Jefferson Airplane, the Byrds, the Doors, Country Joe and the Fish, the 5th Dimension, Canned Heat, the Steve Miller Blues Band, and Moby Grape.

The Hells Angels acted as unofficial security and motorcycled some of the performers up the mountain, including driving a very drunk Jim Morrison of the Doors onto the stage of Mount Tam's Mountain Theater.

The crowd of thirty-five thousand completely overwhelmed the venue's capacity.

The Monterey Pop Festival happened a week later and with its movie, *Monterey Pop*, eclipsed the Tam festival. The Jefferson Airplane brought down the house, Janis Joplin with Big Brother knocked everybody out with "Ball and Chain," Jimi Hendrix put on his amazing show, and the Who finished its set by triggering smoke bombs as Pete Townsend smashed his guitar.

Woodstock was merely a glint on the horizon, still more than two years away.

To capitalize on the Summer of Love, the Fillmore Auditorium opened six nights a week. The week after Monterey, Bill's show at the Fillmore featured the Airplane as the headliner with Jimi Hendrix as the opening act. On the second night Bill realized that Jimi Hendrix was connecting with the audience in extraordinary ways and transforming the concert experience into something unique.

Bill judged artists largely by their live performances and impact on the audiences. Bill considered Hendrix, Janis Joplin, and Jim Morrison as some of the few elite live performers. He thought of Janis as erupting like volcano on the stage, but observed, "You were watching a candle burn, with no wax to replace what had already been used up."

The Summer of Love was now a thing, and throngs of young people answered the call and came to San Francisco. The new youth culture was on full display, but the innocence would not last.

WHERE HAVE ALL THE FLOWERS GONE

THE YEAR 1968 WAS one of upheaval. Martin Luther King, Jr., and Bobby Kennedy were assassinated. Later that summer, large protests were held at the Democratic National Convention, and the Chicago 7 were arrested along with Bobby Seale of the Black Panthers.

Love in the Haight disappeared as runaways, homelessness, and hard drugs overwhelmed the area. Initially the neighborhood had seemed to offer love and freedom, but within months it had become a sordid, mean drug scene.

To capture the ever-increasing crowds wanting to attend his musical events, Bill opened larger venues: Winterland and Fillmore West in San Francisco and Fillmore East in New York City. The era of the intimate Fillmore Auditorium was finished. Bill closed the Fillmore on July 4, 1968, just two years after he had opened it and created its singular experience.

Woodstock happened during the summer of 1969. In December of that year the Altamont Speedway rock concert, featuring the Rolling Stones, took place and became infamous for the brutal stabbing and murder of an audience member by a Hells Angel.

In September of 1970, Jimi Hendrix died, and a month later Janis Joplin followed. Jim Morrison exited this life in Paris in July of 1971. They were all electric as live performers, but it took everything they had and more. All had turned to drugs, alcohol, or both, and each left this earth much too young—at age twenty-seven.

Bill's life, by his own assessment, had become unbalanced. In 1970 his marriage of less than three years to his administrative assistant, Bonnie MacLean, failed, ending in divorce and a battle over custody of their son David. Bill retreated alone to an apartment on Clay Street in San Francisco. His life continued to be dominated by his work.

In 1971 Bill closed both Fillmore East and Fillmore West. But he continued as the country's most prominent rock promoter, putting on larger and larger headline events and tours.

Later in the decade, Bill changed course slightly when he jumped at Francis Ford Coppola's offer of a role in *Apocalypse Now*. It was being filmed in the Philippine jungle, where it was raining all the time. Bill slept on a mat made of hay on a dirt floor. There were no newspapers, no TV, no drugs, and no decent food.

Bill's contract entitled him to a salary of only two dollars per day. But it required the film company to fly him by helicopter every other day into a small village with a public phone so that he could negotiate and do business with acts back in the U.S. and abroad.

In his jungle isolation Bill began examining who he was, what he was doing, and what his future held. He realized that he was conducting his business life in ways he did not like, battling all the time to make money. He decided he would take matters into his own hands and do not what was expected of him, but what he wanted to do.

Bill closed Winterland in 1978. He had opened it immediately following the Summer of Love, but it was now out of phase with the mega concerts that rock bands were demanding. With a capacity of 5400 people, Winterland had been a good size for listening to the music and still feeling part of the scene. But the communal element, the camaraderie at concerts had vanished. Concerts had become more of a commodity experience, just something that people bought.

Bill devoted a lot of time to promoting huge benefit concerts world-wide to support causes he believed in. He also promoted concerts for various band tours, including those for the Rolling Stones.

But just as the magic of the sixties had disappeared over time, Bill's own enjoyment seemed to vanish over the years. He missed bringing performing artists to a more intimate venue and creating a magical connection with the audience.

In 1989 Bill lost out to a competitor on the promotion of the Rolling Stones tour and became seriously depressed. He identified three sources of his depression: his problems in creating long-term relationships with the women in his life, a fire that had burned down his office, and a deepening dissatisfaction with his recent business career. He wanted to do new things—things not driven by money.

In 1991 he turned sixty, and by then his optimism had returned. He was in a satisfying personal relationship with Melissa Gold, and the two were spending almost all their time together. She was an activist in civic affairs, and she and Bill had begun their relationship about a year previously after working together on plans to welcome Nelson Mandela to San Francisco. Bill's usual energy and vitality had returned, and he was enjoying life again.

On October 25, 1991, Bill awoke happy in his Mill Valley home and put in a routine day at the office. He telephoned Mick Jagger, who was in France, but missed him.

That afternoon at Novato's Gnoss Field, Bill and Melissa hopped on a helicopter piloted by Steve Kahn and flew to the Concord Pavilion for a Huey Lewis show. On the return flight after the show, the helicopter ran into a power pole just west of Vallejo and exploded. Bill, Melissa, and Steve all died.

People were stunned, and Bill's passing was lamented throughout the rock world.

The following weekend, on November 3, Bill's life was celebrated with a free concert in Golden Gate Park before an audience of 300,000. The Grateful Dead, Santana, Crosby, Stills, Nash and Young, John Fogerty, Journey, Robin Williams, and others performed. Bill had probably argued with every one of them at one time or another, but he had always poured his heart into promoting their careers. And they knew that he had always done everything he could, down to the last detail, to enhance their performances and the audience's enjoyment of them.

As for the sixties, they lived on, embedded in a generation's attitude that endured long after the exterior symbols of the era had disappeared.

The protests against the war and the draft had made a difference. The pill had brought about a different sexual reality. But it was the freedom of thought, unrestricted by former convention, that defined the Sixties.

The sixties were not monolithic—they happened in different ways in different places at different times, seen always through the lens of the viewer. But if you are old enough to remember the sixties, you cannot recall them without the sounds of rock 'n' roll floating through your mind. It might be a certain performance of a band, a special song, or a dance to the beat, but it will be there.

For rock 'n' roll was more than a soundtrack. It was the anthem of the sixties, and Bill Graham played a huge part in making it so.

The Prison Escape Artist

THE PRISON ESCAPE ARTIST

FORREST TUCKER HAD BARELY passed through San Quentin's gates in October of 1978 when he began his escape. During his reception interview the fifty-eight-year-old Tucker falsely stated his occupation as "boat builder." The lie worked, and Tucker was assigned to work in the prison's furniture factory next to San Francisco Bay's waters. From there he would soon engineer San Quentin's most flamboyant and stylish escape.

Tucker's actual profession was bank robber. He was backstopped by a second skill—he was the country's best at escaping from prison. As he recounted in jailhouse interviews for a 2003 *New Yorker* profile, "It did not matter to me if they gave me five years, ten years, or life. I was an escape artist."

In a sense, Tucker spent much of his life training for his San Quentin escape. Sent in 1936 at age fifteen to a Florida jail for stealing a car, Tucker bolted as soon as his chains were removed and outraced his guard to freedom. "At fifteen, you're pretty fast," he recalled.

After several days the sheriff captured Tucker in an orange grove, where he was snacking on the fruit. This time the sheriff sent him directly to reform school. Tucker had prepared for that earlier by passing some hacksaw blades and a chisel to a couple of friends inside. During his first night of confinement, Tucker used the tools to cut his way out, helping his two friends escape at the same time.

He fled to Georgia but was soon recaptured and sentenced to confinement and labor on a chain gang. Tucker spent most of the next several years in prison for various crimes.

When he was paroled at age twenty-four, he decided to try out the law abiding life. He attempted a career in music, playing his saxophone in big bands. He married briefly and had a daughter, Gaile. But neither his music career nor his marriage worked out, and Tucker returned to a life of crime. Many years later, while on the lam, he would call upon daughter Gaile for help.

Tucker first pursued the profession of bank robber in September of 1950. With gun drawn and a handkerchief covering his face, Tucker robbed a Miami bank of $1278. Bank robbery would become his addiction. When prison prevented him from feeding that addiction, he resorted to his alternative fix—that of escape.

After his successful first bank holdup, Tucker made the rookie mistake of robbing the same bank just days later. He was arrested by the side of the road trying to open a small safe he had grabbed in the heist. He was convicted and sent to prison—for Tucker only a temporary obstacle.

A couple of months later, he faked severe abdominal pain and pleaded with prison guards for treatment. He was taken to a hospital where the doctors diagnosed him with appendicitis and performed surgery. To Tucker it was "a small price to pay," for he escaped during his recovery by picking the lock chaining him to his hospital bed. He strolled out of the hospital unnoticed and made his way to California and freedom.

Although he was adept at picking locks and handy with tools, Tucker's escapes ultimately relied upon his uncanny ability to exploit human error. He used psychological misdirection rather than violence to exit his prisons and especially loved the challenge of the contest with prison personnel. To him it was all "a game, a game to outwit the authorities."

In California, Tucker clothed his life in suburban normalcy while continuing to rob banks. He married Shirley Storz in June of 1951 under the assumed name of Richard Bellow, who was actually Tucker's accomplice in several of his California bank robberies. The newly-wed couple lived in a nice apartment in San Mateo. In October of 1952, Shirley bore him a son, whom they named Richard Jr.

Several months later, the FBI arrested Tucker at his safe deposit box in San Francisco. The agents then drove to his San Mateo apartment and questioned Shirley, who had never heard of Forrest Tucker. She told them she was married to Richard Bellow, a successful songwriter. When shown a photograph of Tucker, she broke down. "I can't believe it," she said. "He was such a good man, such a good provider."

Thirty-three-year-old Tucker was sentenced to thirty years on "the Rock," Alcatraz. A few weeks after he began his sentence, his wife visited him. She told him that they were finished, that she would go it alone. Tucker agreed: "The best thing you can do is make a life for you and our son. I won't bother you no matter what, no matter how much I want to. I won't ring your phone."

He never did see or talk to her again. Yet many years later in his jailhouse interview sessions he said, "We loved each other. I didn't know how to explain to her the truth—that this was my way of life."

Once Tucker was imprisoned on Alcatraz, he began putting an escape plan in motion. He planted just enough steel wool on various prisoners to set off the prison metal detectors. Soon the prison guards began to disregard the beeping machines, allowing Tucker and two other inmates to smuggle in the tools they needed.

Their plan was to tunnel through the floor to the basement and from there flee to freedom, a scheme foiled only when another prisoner informed on them. The prison authorities searched the fingered prisoners' cells and discovered their tools, including a blowtorch, a bar spreader, and cutters, all puttied inside hollows carved into their toilet bowls.

In 1956 Tucker made a second escape attempt. He stabbed himself intentionally with a broken pencil and was taken to an outside hospital for treatment. While proceeding to the X-ray room, he pushed aside his guards and fled the hospital. He was free for several hours before they caught him in a cornfield, still in handcuffs and hospital gown. He spent the following two decades in prison before he was finally released.

Back in society, Tucker returned to his life of bank robbery. In the autumn of 1978, he was captured following his hold-up of a Sacramento bank and was sentenced to seven years in San Quentin.

RUB-A-DUB-DUB, THREE MEN IN A TUB

ONCE ASSIGNED TO A work detail in San Quentin's furniture factory, Tucker recruited two other inmates, John Waller and William McGirk, for his next escape attempt. Over the following months the three gathered scraps of wood, Formica, and Masonite which they shaped and hid under tarps. From the electrical shop, they took poles and buckets. From the furniture factory warehouse they pilfered plastic furniture dust covers and tape and stored them in boxes labeled "Office Supplies."

They routinely lunched by the bay in preparation for their escape. They noted the Marin Yacht Club's signature orange color, and they calculated the timing of the tides.

Over time they stealthily constructed pre-fab parts for their escape boat, which they assembled behind a false wall of boxes that they piled high in the furniture factory warehouse. They bolted and taped the boat's wooden frame together, wrapped it with waterproof plastic dust covers, and attached the craft's exterior. Fully assembled the boat was fourteen feet long and thirty inches wide, resembling a cross between a canoe and a kayak.

They painted their sweatshirts and blue prison hats a bright orange to match the color often worn by Marin Yacht Club members. Though they managed to smuggle in a deep-blue spray paint to adorn the boat, they had only enough to cover one side. They sprayed it on the boat's right side—the one that would face the prison guard towers on their planned escape route.

Tucker was determined to put a final stylish flourish in place. Ignoring hurry-up pleas from his cohorts, he stenciled the boat with the name he had chosen: "Rub-A-Dub-Dub."

On August 9, 1979, Tucker signaled his two confederates that they were ready. From the prison grounds they launched the boat unseen into the bay and headed west along the shoreline toward the Larkspur Ferry Terminal. The afternoon winds were strong, more than twenty miles per hour.

The boat proved to be water tight, but the waves were pouring over its side as they paddled past the tall guard tower closest to the bay. The unsuspecting tower guard asked if they needed help. They assured him things were fine, and he went back to his duties.

By the time they reached the prison's western boundary, the boat was close to capsizing. The officer at the west gate and the patrol officer, who had just arrived there in his vehicle, called out to the floundering men not knowing they were convicts. The drenched boaters assured them that their wives were waiting for them with a meal and change of clothes. One of the escapees—either Waller or McGirk—held up his arm and looking at his bare wrist jested, "It's okay. My Timex is still ticking." The guards laughed and resumed their routines.

Just past the prison's grounds the boat overturned, spilling the inmates into the bay. They grabbed on to the boat, held on, and swam it ashore. They beached it beyond the prison boundary and vanished, each going his separate way. The empty boat was discovered less than an hour later.

The warden was quickly alerted to the escape, and he summoned Dick Nelson, the prison personnel assistant, to his office. The warden instructed Nelson to pull the keys to the furniture factory warehouse, inspect it carefully for clues, and report back. He was to keep everyone else out of the warehouse and retain the set of keys until advised otherwise.

Nelson entered the warehouse, searched it carefully, and discovered the false wall of boxes. He explored behind the boxes and was shocked to see the escape boat's ragged outline spray-painted in blue on the floor.

The escape was successful for months until McGirk was captured in San Rafael on October 30 1979. The authorities caught up with Waller in Gilroy on April 13 1980.

The Marin County District Attorney tried McGirk and Waller twice for escape, a crime generally without any defense. After all, either you escaped or you didn't. The jury deadlocked both times, the second time

8–4 for conviction. Some of the jurors apparently admired the imaginative, nonviolent escape and felt there was no need to pile more time on top of the inmates' existing sentences. After the two prosecution failures, the D.A. declined to try McGirk and Waller a third time.

Tucker remained at large. According to his daughter Gaile's account some forty years later, Tucker telephoned her for help after his San Quentin escape. He told her, "Honey, I'm going to be flying into Miami Airport. I'll be in disguise. Will you pick me up?"

At the airport she recognized her father, who was disguised as a pensioner with a beard, black hat, and cane. She drove him to her home and allowed him to use it briefly as a safe house.

She generally saw him only when he was on the run. As she commented in her retrospective account, "I realize he loved my brother Rick and [me], but he loved robbing banks and escaping more. That was his life; that came first."

Tucker continued to elude the authorities until September 1981, when he was arrested in a downtown Boston department store for credit card fraud. But communication between the California and Massachusetts authorities about Tucker's escape and unserved San Quentin sentence somehow went awry. As a result, the Massachusetts court was unaware of Tucker's California past and ordered bail of $2500 for his credit card crime only. A woman posted bail and—poof!—Tucker was free again.

Tucker used his new freedom to assemble a criminal gang of well-dressed oldsters. For the next year or so, his crew—which authorities dubbed the "Over-The-Hill-Gang"—pulled off some sixty bank heists in Texas and Oklahoma and are believed to have pulled off several other robberies elsewhere. Witnesses described the gang members as older gentlemen, but focused particularly on one of them—it was Tucker—who wore a large hearing aid. Tucker's hearing aid was much more than that. Attached by a wire through his shirt to a police scanner, it allowed Tucker to monitor silent alarms or other alerts to the police and to direct his gang accordingly.

One lawman who futilely pursued the gang admitted: "They were the most professional, successful robbers that I ever encountered in all my years on the force. They had more experience in robbery than we had catching them."

During a break from his bank robbery duties, Tucker met Jewell Centers, a wealthy, attractive Florida widow. Masquerading as a stockbroker named Bob Callahan, Tucker married her in June of 1982.

The marriage did not domesticate Tucker. By 1983 he was plotting his largest-ever robbery, one that depended on his talent for outwitting his adversaries. His scheme was to intercept a scheduled transfer of cash from a Massachusetts high-security bank to an armored truck. The trick would be to accomplish the heist without any notice to law enforcement until Tucker and his accomplices were long gone.

Tucker planned the heist carefully. He and his gang cased the bank for some time, registering the dates and times of the scheduled armored truck pickups and the procedures employed. They noted the exterior look of the armored truck and the dress of its personnel.

On March 7, 1983, just minutes before a scheduled cash pick up, the gang members impersonating armored truck employees entered the bank and were escorted to the vault by the bank manager and two tellers. They picked up the cash, locked the manager and tellers in the vault, and exited the bank with more than $430,000.

The getaway was clean. But three months later when Tucker attempted to visit the Florida home of an accomplice and long-time friend, he was recognized by FBI agents staking out the premises. When he tried to flee, they shot him in his arms and a leg. Tucker hijacked a car, but the agents caught up to him a few miles away. He was lying by the side of the road, unconscious from loss of blood.

His wife, Jewell Centers, was shocked when informed by the FBI that Bob Callahan, her successful stock broker husband, was actually Forrest Tucker, a notorious bank robber. But Jewell had greatly enjoyed Tucker's company during their marriage, and unlike Tucker's previous two wives, she waited for him.

In his Miami jail cell Tucker, then sixty-four, shifted to his backup profession and went to work. He sawed through a cell bar, squeezed out, and used a homemade grappling hook to climb to the roof. But that was as far as he got.

Florida authorities captured Tucker and, relieved to be rid of him, sent him to California to serve out his San Quentin sentence. Inmates reveled in stories of his escape and dubbed him "Captain." This time though, rather than attempting escape, Tucker used a flurry of appeals to reduce his sentence. He was released in 1993 at the age of seventy-three.

He moved back in with his wife Jewell Centers and settled into an affluent country-club life in Pompano Beach, Florida, where he engaged in various artistic pursuits. He penned a book draft detailing his life of crime and prison escapes. He set up a music room and gave saxophone and clarinet lessons for $25 an hour. He composed music for his wife and every once in a while played at local jazz clubs. Outwardly, Tucker was leading a comfortable, fulfilling life. Inwardly, he hungered for the creative challenges and adrenaline rush of his criminal lifestyle.

After more than four years of lawful comfort, Tucker could stand it no more. In 1998 he successfully robbed four Florida banks.

The next year, at age seventy-eight, Tucker pulled off his last robbery. Dressed stylishly in all white with white suede shoes and a white ascot pulled up over his face, he entered a bank in Jupiter, Florida, brandishing an old Army Colt 45. He walked up to a teller and asked her politely to put all her money on the counter. As she placed the bundles of bills in front of him, he inspected them for exploding dye.

He repeated the process with a second teller, then collected the money and, ever the gentleman, graciously thanked both tellers as he left.

Tucker drove his stolen getaway car to a nearby location where he had stowed his swap car, an untraceable red Pontiac Grand Am. From the getaway car he removed the packets of cash and his bank-robbing tools, including a .357 Magnum, a sawed-off .30 Carbine, a police badge, and a police scanner, and placed them all in the Grand Am. He wiped down the getaway car to remove his fingerprints, checked to make sure he had his heart medicine, and drove away in the Grand Am.

No one seemed to be pursuing him, and he stopped to count the money, violating the Kenny Rogers song admonition not to "count your money" till "the dealin's done." He thumbed through the bills, stacked his take of more than $5000 beside him, and headed for home. As he drove, he noticed an unmarked car tailing him and then a police car.

He tried to lose them but was soon blocked by a dead-end street. He turned his car around, only to confront a police car broadside in the road and an officer reaching for his shotgun.

Tucker accelerated and aimed the Grand Am for a small gap between the police car and a neighboring fence. He lost control of the car, and it hurtled over an embankment and smashed into a palm tree. The car's air bags ballooned, pinning the white-haired seventy-eight-year-old Tucker to his seat.

He was sentenced to thirteen years at the federal prison in Fort Worth, Texas. There, in late 2002, Tucker gave jailhouse interviews to David Grann for a profile in *The New Yorker*. He gave no other interviews because he wanted to sell his life story to Hollywood for a movie scripted from his book draft.

Tucker failed to sell his book or generate any interest from the movie studios, but in 2018 (far too late for Tucker to enjoy) his cinema dreams were realized courtesy of Robert Redford. With Redford both directing and starring, Tucker was immortalized (with the usual cinematic license) in "The Old Man & the Gun." The film, based on the New Yorker profile, focused primarily on Tucker's later years.

In his jailhouse interviews, Tucker boasted of escaping successfully eighteen times and compiled a list of all eighteen, followed by a hopeful "19" left blank. He was never able to fill it in.

Forrest Tucker died in prison in 2004, unable to escape life's ultimate sentence.

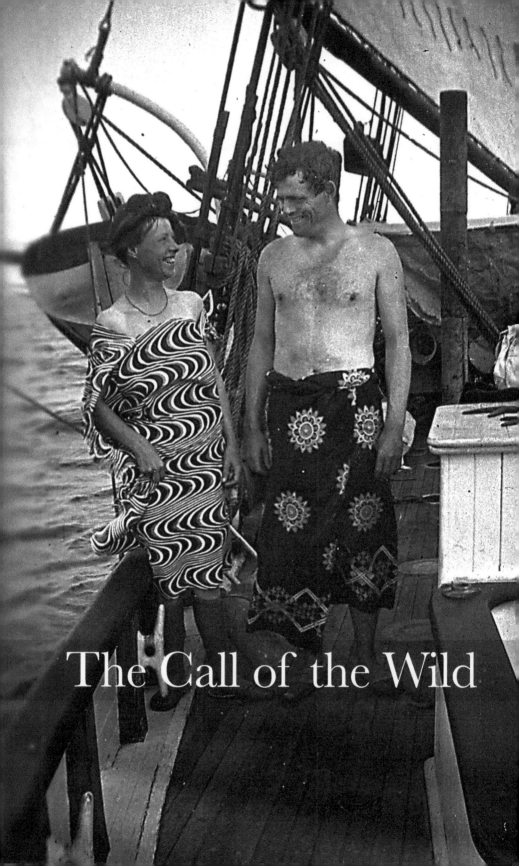

The Call of the Wild

THE CALL OF THE WILD

THERE ARE METEORS IN the sky but few on Earth, and Jack London was one. Born into poverty, he worked several jobs during elementary school, leaving school at age eleven. He toiled at a cannery until he quit at age 15 to become an oyster pirate in San Francisco Bay.

After his pirate days, he worked on a schooner, rode the rails and tramped the United States, searched for gold in the Klondike, reported on Japan's war with Russia, sailed the Pacific for two years, and ranched in Sonoma County.

Along the way he wrote fifty books—including several famed novels and many short stories—and became in his time the country's most popular writer. But Jack's own life was his greatest tale.

He was born on January 12, 1876, as John Griffith Chaney. His father was listed on the birth certificate as W. H. Chaney, but he had deserted Jack's mother, Flora Wellman, months earlier and always denied paternity. Eight months after Jack's birth, Flora married John London, and Jack became Jack London.

Jack's childhood was grim. In his description: ". . . I had no child-hood. Up at three o'clock in the morning to carry papers. When that was finished I did not go home but continued on to school. School out, my evening papers. Saturday I worked on an ice wagon. Sunday I went to a bowling alley and set up pins for drunken Dutchman. Duty—I turned over every cent and went dressed like a scarecrow."

After he left school at age eleven, he began to labor at a cannery. He recalled: ". . . I was up and at work at six in the morning. . . . I worked every night till ten, eleven and twelve o'clock. . . . My body and soul were starved when I was a child."

Astonishingly, his childhood did not beat him down but quickened in him a fierce fire and hunger for a life of adventure and accomplishment. He described himself as "Hungry! Hungry! Hungry! From the time I stole the meat and knew no call above my belly, to now when the call is higher, it has been hunger, nothing but hunger."

OYSTER PIRATE

AFTER THE ALL-CONSUMING DRUDGERY of his early years, Jack "wanted to be where the winds of adventure blew. And the winds of adventure blew the oyster pirate sloops up and down San Francisco Bay."

At age fifteen he became a pirate, sailing the bay in darkness to raid the guarded oyster beds. He risked getting shot or jailed, but to him that was of little consequence: "The men in stripes worked a shorter day than I at my machine. And there was vastly more romance in being an oyster pirate or a convict than in being a machine slave."

The oyster pirates were a rough crew of brawling, drinking men and to be accepted Jack had to join them with abandon. He discarded the thrifty spending habits of his poverty days, and treated everyone to drinks with a reckless generosity. He enjoyed the "glorious company of free souls" and was initiated into manhood by the Queen of the Oyster Pirates. He reveled in "the smack and slap of the spirit of revolt, of adventure, of romance, of the things forbidden and done defiantly and grandly."

As a young boy he had become comfortable on the water, first in a small leaky rowboat he had purchased for $2 and later in a skiff he had sailed out into the bay. By the time he ventured into piracy he was an expert sailor.

Early in his piracy days he borrowed $300 to purchase his own pirate sloop, the *Razzle Dazzle*. He often manned it alone, challenging intruders with a cocked double-barreled shotgun while he steered with his feet.

Drink was always a part of the pirating life, and Jack began to equate booze with adventure and comradery. In later years alcohol would become a serious issue for him, but at the time he was young, strong, and resilient and generally recovered quickly from his binges.

After a while he left pirating and switched sides, joining the Fish Patrol which protected the oyster beds and arrested the oyster pirates. He worked areas not frequented by his pirate acquaintances so that he was never forced to confront his old pals.

After a short time, he quit the Fish Patrol. He was just sixteen years old, living on the waterfront and spending most of his time in saloons. He had little education, the beginnings of a drinking problem, and a future that appeared to be unpromising.

That summer he was offered a decent sum to retrieve a friend's stolen boat. Close to Sacramento he encountered a pack of kids who were hoboing, begging, and stealing to survive. They were riding the rails, ducking the bulls (the railroad cops), and living a life on the move that excited Jack.

He gave the life a quick try, grabbing a freight train out of Sacramento and riding it over the hill—the Sierra—into Truckee. He found that he liked the hobo life.

But after his months of piracy and a glimpse of hoboing, he wanted to experience adventures in the world beyond the Golden Gate. Eight days after his seventeenth birthday, he hired on as a seaman on a schooner headed for the Bering Sea to hunt seals.

On the voyage Jack saw the horrors of skinning slaughtered seals, lived through a typhoon, and went ashore in Japan for an epic bout of drinking. When he returned from his time at sea to the Oakland waterfront, his oyster pirate friends had vanished. They were dead, in prison, on the lam, or just gone.

In need of money, he landed a job at a jute mill paying only ten cents an hour. His sole salvation during the period was winning the *San Francisco Call's* writing contest and its prize of $25 for his "Story of a Typhoon Off the Coast of Japan," based on his experience at sea. It was his first published story.

Aspiring next to be an electrician, he applied for a job at the power plant of Oakland's electric railway. The plant manager promised him advancement to electrician but told him he would have to start at the bottom. Jack began by shoveling coal seven days a week with one day off per month, at a monthly salary of $30. He labored for months before a kind employee told him he was being duped—that Jack was replacing two men who had each been making $40 per month.

Jack decided that "learning a trade could go hang. It was a whole lot better to roister and frolic over the world in the way I had previously done. So I headed out on the adventure path again."

TRAMPING

ESCAPE HAS ALWAYS BEEN an American tradition. To avoid being civilized, Huckleberry Finn lit out for the territory. Jack Kerouac set out for adventure on the road and made it famous. Jack's itch was to ride the rails: "I became a tramp—well, because of the life that was in me, of the wanderlust in my blood that would not let me rest."

At the time large groups of the unemployed were gathering in locations throughout the country and traveling to Washington D.C. to pressure Congress to remedy the situation. Jack had planned on riding the rails with the Oakland contingent, but they had already departed by the time he arrived at the depot. Attempting to catch up with them, he hopped a passenger train, jumped an overnight freight, and then grabbed several others heading east.

He finally caught up with a group in Iowa, but after staying with them a while—riding the rails and floating with them on a boat down a stretch of the Mississippi—he left and went his own direction. While tramping Jack had learned how to "throw his feet"—that is, beg for food—to sustain himself. He later credited it with teaching him how to tell a good story.

Eventually he made his way to Niagara Falls, where he spent his first evening sightseeing. In the morning he was arrested for vagrancy and sentenced to thirty days in prison. He was just eighteen years old.

The thirty days he spent in the Erie County Penitentiary he described "as living hell." After his release he continued tramping the

East Coast, noting particularly the wretched poverty of the slums.

Jack later assayed his situation at the time: "I had been born in the working class, and I was now at the age of eighteen, beneath the point at which I had started. I was down in the cellar of society . . ." In another assessment he admitted: "I saw the picture of the Social Pit as vividly as though it were a concrete thing, and at the bottom of the Pit I saw [myself] hanging on to the slippery wall by main strength and sweat. And I confess a terror seized me."

Jack decided "to sell no more muscle, and to become a vendor of brains." Although he had never attended high school, Jack had been addicted to reading from his early days in grammar school: "I read mornings, afternoons, and nights. I read in bed, I read at the table, I read as I walked to and from school, and I read at recess while the other boys were playing."

Still, he felt he had missed out on an education, and at age nineteen he enrolled as a freshman at Oakland High School. After going slightly more than a year, he dropped out and crammed for three months on his own, hoping to gain admission to the University of California at Berkeley. He passed the university's admission exams and began attending classes in August of 1896 but was forced to withdraw in early 1897 to help support his family.

For a few weeks he tried to earn money by writing, receiving nothing but rejections. Next, he worked briefly in a laundry at a boarding school on the San Francisco Peninsula. After that he vowed never to be a "work-beast" again.

THE KLONDIKE

IMMEDIATELY UPON THE FIRST news of a gold strike in the Klondike, Jack and his brother-in-law James Shephard decided to join the stampede of gold seekers hurrying to get there. Shephard, who was married to Jack's step-sister Eliza, paid for both of their boat passages, prospecting gear, and stash of food to sustain them over the Yukon's harsh winter.

On July 25, 1898, Jack and Shephard crammed themselves onto an overcrowded ship heading from San Francisco to Port Townsend, Washington and next caught a boat to Juneau, Alaska. There with three other men they hired some indigenous families with a seventy-foot canoe hollowed out of a large tree trunk to paddle them and their gear the hundred miles up a natural fjord called the Lynn Canal to Dyea.

When they arrived, the beach at Dyea was bedlam. Thousands of gold seekers were scrambling to assemble their outfits from chaotic heaps. The typical outfit weighed about a thousand pounds. It included perhaps seven hundred pounds of food—barely enough to last the Klondike winter—plus tents, sleds, mining tools, and other necessities.

The overhang of winter was threatening the frenzied hordes on one end, while gold was beckoning them on the other. Awaiting them immediately was the hellish climb over Chilkoot Pass, which caused many to fall by the wayside and turn back.

The Chilkoot Trail was called "the worst trail this side of hell," a life-sucking thirty-two miles over the pass to a lake on the other side. One of Jack's partners paid to have his outfit portaged to the pass summit. The others of the group could not afford to pay and carried their own outfits.

Jack and his group began the climb on August 12. Each separated out the heaviest load he could carry and humped it uphill a distance—often less than a mile—to that night's campsite. There they would unload it, and then dodging the uphill climbers, bushwhack down to grab another load. They repeated the process as many times as necessary, while one man remained at each end to guard the packs.

Besides his own outfit, Jack also carried Shephard's in exchange for his payment of Jack's initial expenses. After less than a week on the trail, Shephard was physically unable to continue and decided to return to Oakland.

On August 30, after eighteen days of upward slog, Jack's group finally reached the summit of Chilkoot Pass. Everyone was drenched and cold from the driving rain and totally exhausted. Jack later wrote that at the summit he "would have given a year's income for a fire and a cup of coffee."

The route down from the Pass was a quagmire of mud, bogs and snowfields. As Jack described it: "Men broke their hearts and backs and wept beside the trail. . . . But winter never faltered."

On September 8 they reached the end of the Chilkoot Trail at Lake Lindemann. There Jack and his group teamed up with another group to construct two boats, one for each party. The boats were built with care for they needed to traverse six hundred miles and some perilous water to reach Dawson, where most of the gold seekers were wintered. Each boat was approximately twenty–seven feet long and designed to carry five men plus their heavy outfits.

They set sail at noon on September 21, well aware they were in a race with winter's icing of the waterways. After three days of easy travel, they reached the fearsome waters of Box Canyon. The group eyed the perilous stretch from shore and decided to run it. Many gold seekers watched as the boat, with Jack at the helm, successfully rode through the canyon's boiling waters. Two more life-threatening rapids followed, which they managed to ride successfully before reaching friendly waters.

The blasts of winter chased them to Split-Up Island, one of a group of islands scattered on the Yukon River. The name, Split-Up Island, was attributed to the frequency with which partners separated there, no longer able to stand the close confinement with each other over the long winter.

Jack and a couple of his group decided to stay there, rather than travel the remaining eighty miles to crowded Dawson, and moved into a vacant cabin on the island. The island offered them the added opportunity of finding gold in the nearby Stewart River or Henderson Creek areas, which were not yet saturated with prospectors. Behind them winter had already shut down Chilkoot Pass.

After they settled in, Jack and his companions prospected the surrounding areas and found small amounts of gold. Jack staked out his mining claim to about six acres spanning five hundred feet of Henderson Creek's stream bed and the land on either side from "rimrock to rimrock." On October 16 Jack and two friends boarded their boat for Dawson to record their mining claims officially and to see for themselves the fabled settlement.

After two days on the river, they arrived at the town. There were cabins and tents crammed everywhere to house Dawson's six thousand inhabitants. The Mounties had posted a prominent notice warning those without ample food:

> For those who have not laid in a winter's supply to remain longer is to court death from starvation, or at least the certainty of sickness from scurvy and other troubles. Starvation now stares everyone in the face who is hoping and waiting for outside relief.

Jack officially filed his mining claim only after he had spent eighteen days in Dawson, suggesting that he had scant faith it. The Klondike made Jack rich—but only with stories, not with gold.

After another month in Dawson, Jack and a companion traveled back to Split-up Island, spending five days on the trail to get there. Upon their return the "islands were silent and white. No animals nor humming insects broke the silence. No birds flew in the chill air. . . . The world slept, and it was like the sleep of death."

Much of Jack's time on Split-Up Island was spent waiting out the Arctic winter. Food was limited, consisting largely of the three B's: bread, beans, and bacon. In the consuming darkness, inhabitants concentrated mostly on the temperature and the slow march of time.

Jack's favorite occupation over the winter was conversation. One friend remembered him as good natured, expounding ideas and listening eagerly. Another noted: "To him there was in all things something new, something alluring, something worthwhile . . . He was always on tiptoe with expectancy."

One day in the middle of winter, Jack used a cabin mate's axe and dulled it, causing a dispute between them. Jack felt it necessary to switch cabins, confirming the aptness of Split-Up Island's name.

He moved in with three men, including Doc Harvey, known for his tall tales. According to Jack, any exaggerations regarding the Klondike "could not stretch the truth as fast as the truth itself stretched." Men could continue to tell lies, "but the truth could continue to outrun them."

During the Yukon's long winter, Jack was keenly aware of the overwhelming and stupefying "White Silence." By May the silence had vanished as sunlight and warmth jabbed, cracked, and popped the ice.

By then Jack and many others were afflicted by scurvy caused by a lack of vitamin C—they had no fruits or vegetables, even in dried or canned form, to prevent it.

Jack's scurvy had made his gums spongy, loosened his teeth, and severely weakened his legs. Doc Harvey warned Jack that unless cured of his scurvy, he would go lame, his eyes would recede into their sockets, and he would die.

As soon as the ice began to thaw, Jack and Doc Harvey built a raft. When the Yukon River became navigable, they pushed off from Split-Up Island and headed for Dawson to find aid for their scurvy. They landed in late May towing a huge pile of logs behind them, which they sold, along with the raft's logs, for the considerable sum of $600.

Then they hurried to seek treatment for their scurvy at the hospital in Dawson established by Father William Judge, "the saint of Dawson." After doing what he could, Father Judge advised Jack to get to civilization and fresh fruits and vegetables as quickly as possible.

Jack and two other men departed Dawson in a "home-made, weak-kneed and leaky" rowboat to travel the two thousand miles downstream to the Bering Sea coast. As they left, Jack looked back for the last time on "dreary, desolate Dawson."

The midnight sun was ascendant, and the men decided to travel around the clock. Jack and another man took twelve-hour shifts at the tiller and the third man cooked and otherwise assisted. Jack took the tiller from midnight to noon, a shift familiar to him from his oyster pirate days.

In his account "From Dawson to the Sea," Jack described the striking beauty and charm of their drift down the Yukon with its "overhanging forest, the smell of the land and the damp warmth of vegetation. And above all, the hum of life, bursting into sudden gushes of song, slowly swelling to a great, dull roar of satisfaction or dying away into sweetly cadenced silence."

Their float downriver was not all peace and serenity as the group was under incessant attack from mosquitoes. One of the men claimed that he had watched as the insects avoided their mosquito netting, "one gang holding up the edge while a second gang crawled under."

On the evening of June 18 they reached Anvik, where Jack received some help for his scurvy. By then his condition was dire. In his diary he confided that his scurvy had "almost entirely crippled me from my waist down. Right leg drawn up, can no longer straighten it, even in walking must put my whole weight on toes."

Receiving a can of tomatoes and some fresh potatoes in Anvik, he wrote gratefully in his diary: "These few raw potatoes & tomatoes are worth more to me at the present stage of the game than an El Dorado claim."

From Anvik Jack's skilled seamanship carried them to St. Michaels on the Bering Sea. Jack departed St. Michaels on a steamship, having agreed to stoke coal in exchange for passage. His diary's final entry revealed his sentiments: "Leave St. Michaels—unregrettable moment." He arrived in San Francisco in July 1898, almost exactly a year after he had left.

In many ways it was the year that made him. As Jack wrote later, "It was in the Klondike that I found myself. . . . You get your true perspective. I got mine."

BREAKTHROUGH

UPON HIS RETURN, JACK learned that John London, the only father he had ever known, had died. Jack felt a need to earn money and first tried writing, flooding the market with anything he thought might sell. Unsuccessful in those efforts, he took on various odd jobs to tide himself over and applied for a job with the post office.

The *Overland Monthly*, a magazine based in San Francisco, ultimately accepted one of his stories, "To the Man on the Trail," and offered a pittance of $5 for it. Jack reluctantly agreed to it.

It was a difficult time for Jack. He wrote to a friend "About the loneliest Christmas I ever faced." On New Year's Eve he confessed to another, "I have never been so hard up in my life."

In January salvation arrived. The editor of *The Black Cat*, a San Francisco magazine, accepted one of Jack's stories and wrote that if Jack would let him cut the story in half, he would send Jack forty dollars. Jack responded that "he could cut down two-halves if he'd only send the money along."

Jack reflected later on the *Black Cat* editor's importance to him: "He saved my literary life, if he did not save my general life. And I think he was guilty of the second crime, too."

Days later the Oakland postmaster called to offer Jack the postal job he had previously applied for. With his writing prospects looking better, Jack asked if he could pass on the present offer but reserve the right to accept the next position available. The postmaster coldly gave him an ultimatum: "Take it or leave it." Jack left it. He later confessed, "I am afraid I always was an extremist."

He threw himself anew into his stories, writing for almost nineteen hours a day. He believed that "a strong will can accomplish anything. . . . There is no such thing as inspiration, and very little of genius." Editors were looking for action stories with no frills or fancy language, and Jack's writing fit the bill exactly.

The Black Cat had saved him financially, but *The Atlantic* gave him prestige. In January of 1900 it published his story, "An Odyssey of the North" and paid him $120 for it.

But Jack was never in it just for the money. He explained, "More money means more life to me. . . . So the habit of money-getting will never become one of my vices. But the habit of money spending, ah God! I shall always be its victim."

On Christmas in 1899 Jack signed a contract with Houghton, Mifflin & Company to publish his book of nine short stories of the North entitled *The Son of the Wolf.* When published the following year, Jack was hailed for his "natural gift for storytelling" and his "refreshing frankness, and touches of poetic insight."

That same year he married Bessie Maddern, a serious woman who he thought was a good companion but did not love. A year later they had a daughter, Joan, and he also ran for mayor of Oakland on the socialist ticket, garnering a scant 245 votes.

In 1902 Jack traveled to London, England and spent six weeks in London's worst slum. He lived a life of inconceivable misery among "the people of the abyss," as he later titled his book about the experience. His second daughter, Becky, was born in October.

The year 1903 changed Jack's life. He fell in love with Charmian Kittredge during the summer and separated from his wife Bessie.

Charmian was four years older than Jack. A liberated woman, she fearlessly availed herself of the freedoms that men were allowed but that convention denied women. She was an excellent athlete and craved adventure.

The romance between Jack and Charmian was sparked in June at the Wake Robin Lodge in Glen Ellen where Jack and his family had rented a vacation cabin for the summer. Charmian was at the lodge to assist her aunt, an owner, and one day delivered some supplies to the Londons' cabin. Jack was there alone, and as she was leaving, he grabbed her and impulsively kissed her.

Jack was just looking for a fling, but within a week he had fallen in love with Charmian and decided that they would live together for life. Jack and Bessie separated soon after, and the newspapers and gossips trumpeted the news.

Still, Charmian and Jack managed to keep their relationship secret. When not seeing each other, they corresponded daily. Jack was effusive in declaring his feelings for Charmian in their letters, calling her his "great, great love!" and telling her ". . . I shall love you forever and forever."

That same year Macmillan published Jack's famous dog adventure novel, *The Call of the Wild*. He had intended to write just a short yarn, Jack explained to his publisher, "but it got away from me." *The Call of the Wild* was—and continues to be—his most popular book, and for a time it made Jack the most widely read author in the United States and perhaps the world.

His books and stories had immediacy and truth. Jack shared with his readers details that could only be acquired from having lived the life, and they gave his tales a gripping authenticity.

In late 1903 the Hearst newspapers sought to capitalize on Jack's wide readership and outbid all others for his services as correspondent to cover the war between Russia and Japan. Jack signed on for the money, but it was the chance for a new adventure that really excited him.

Upon his arrival in Japan in early 1904, he quickly discovered that the Japanese government had no intention of allowing war correspondents anywhere near the actual battles. Without authorization or approval, Jack used his own resources to get to the front and began taking photographs to send back to the Hearst newspapers. The Japanese authorities soon arrested him and confiscated his camera. Fortunately, the U.S. minister to Japan interceded to save both Jack and his camera.

Undeterred by the arrest, Jack chartered a fishing junk and finally reached a small village closer to the front. The inhabitants had never seen a Caucasian before and he was an object of great curiosity—so much so, that one resident woke him at three in the morning to have a confirming look.

From there Jack bluffed his way past military authorities and rode nearly two hundred miles on horseback to move even closer to the action. He suffered through freezing temperatures, festering sores, and lice but finally did witness a skirmish.

Japanese officials soon corralled him and kept him far from the front. In frustration he unwisely punched a Japanese horse groom. He was arrested immediately and held for court-martial by the Japanese military, which was bent on imposing severe punishment.

A fellow correspondent sent an urgent cable to President Theodore Roosevelt informing him of Jack's peril. Roosevelt admired Jack greatly, and cabled the Japanese government demanding his release. With great reluctance the authorities freed him, but they ordered him to return to the United States. It was one of the few orders that Jack happily obeyed.

THE VALLEY OF THE MOON

IN MARCH OF 1905 Jack was suffering through one of his cyclical depressions, telling Charmian, "I don't seem to care for anything—I'm sick. . . . I don't know what I want." He began to emerge from his gloom later that month while horseback riding with Charmian in Sonoma County's Valley of the Moon, and in April they moved there.

He decided to build a home in the valley, and in June contracted to purchase 129 acres of land outside Glen Ellen. To close the purchase, he requested an advance of $10,000 from his publisher, calling the property, "the most beautiful, primitive land to be found anywhere in California."

The purchase and prospects of working the land brought an end to his depression. He wrote later, "Part of the process of recovering from my long sickness was to find delight in little things . . . On the ranch, in the Valley of the Moon, I found my paradise."

Jack and Charmian named their dream place, the "Beauty Ranch." In November they married, and Jack proclaimed he was finally settled. But he was already mapping out their next long adventure.

They planned to travel around the world in a boat they would have built specially, which they later named the "*Snark*." They would sail first to Hawaii and from there to the South Seas.

He sold a magazine publisher on the idea by stating: "We expect lots of action, and my strong point as a writer is that I am a writer of action—see all my short stories, for instance."

TO THE SOUTH SEAS

JACK ABANDONED ALL COMMON sense in building the *Snark*. They could have purchased a seaworthy vessel suitable for their voyage for about $5000. But as in all things, he was somewhat bullheaded and needed to do it himself. By the time the Snark was completed and ready to sail, it had cost six times as much.

After numerous costly and frustrating delays, Jack and Charmian finally set sail on the *Snark* for Hawaii and the South Seas in April of 1907. As they departed through the Golden Gate, hundreds of boats whistled their farewells.

The *Snark* arrived in Honolulu and docked at Pearl Harbor in May after twenty-seven days at sea. Jack and Charmian luxuriated in Hawaii's caresses for five months.

It was in the Hawaiian tropical warmth that Jack wrote his classic story of the frozen North, "To Build a Fire." Its protagonist, a man inexperienced in the ways of the North ignores an old-timer's warning of the Northland code that one must never travel alone when the temperature is lower than fifty degrees below zero. The story recounts the consequences of the man's arrogant disregard of this advice.

With the Arctic story written, Jack took to the warm sand of Waikiki Beach. Looking seaward, he was fascinated by the sight of a fellow riding a board down the curl of the ocean's breaking waves. At the time surfing was little known beyond Hawaii, but Jack was excited to try it.

He labored for a while at mastering the basics, but once he had, his instructor took him out to the deep water where the big waves climbed high. Jack surfed them and exulted in the pure adventure of riding the ocean's primal force.

As a special favor Jack and Charmian were permitted to visit Molokai's leper colony. They spent five days there freely traveling among and mingling with the patients. Jack was sympathetic to the lepers' plight and brought some of that sympathy to his stories about them.

After five months of enjoyment in Hawaii, they departed in early October, taking the difficult traverse across the trade winds to the

Marquesas. From there they traveled to Tahiti and then to a happy ten days in Bora Bora. They did not know it, but their idyllic days were behind them by the time they reached the Solomon Islands.

THE SOLOMON ISLANDS

IN HIS BOOK *The Cruise of the Snark*, Jack's judgment of the Solomon Islands was brutal: "If I were a king, the worst punishment I could inflict on my enemies would be to banish them to the Solomons. On second thought, king or no king, I don't think I'd have the heart to do it."

In the Solomons Jack, Charmian, and the entire crew suffered badly from various afflictions, including malaria, dysentery, and ulcerating sores. In a short story entitled "The Terrible Solomons," Jack related "that fever and dysentery are perpetually on the walk-about, that loathsome skin diseases abound, that the air is saturated with a poison that bites into every pore, cut, or abrasion and plants malignant ulcers, and that many strong men who escape dying there return as wrecks to their own countries."

The islands' inhabitants were also terrifying, for they had "a hearty appetite for human flesh and a fad for collecting human heads." Only a few years earlier a warship bearing the foreboding name of the *Albatross* had ventured to the Solomons, and with two exceptions, the entire crew had been killed and eaten by the islanders.

Matters reached their low point when Jack and Charmian left the *Snark* and boarded a ship engaged in the loathsome business of falsely inducing or kidnapping Solomon Islanders to work on plantations in Australia and elsewhere under conditions amounting to slavery.

The ship ran aground on a reef and was surrounded almost immediately by canoes carrying armed islanders with cartridges and other objects jammed through holes in their ears. The ship, crew, and passengers were now the prey.

The captain was aware of another vessel just five miles away, and wrote a letter pleading for rescue before his ship broke up and they were killed by the islanders. But the letter was useless without a way to deliver it.

The crew offered a half a case of tobacco to any islander in a surrounding canoe willing to transport the message to the other vessel. The islanders were unmoved, anticipating that in a few hours the ship would break up and they would get their tobacco anyway. Finally, the crew persuaded a man in a small canoe to make the trip.

About three hours later the other ship arrived, and its fully armed crew caused the menacing canoes to retreat. It took a couple more days to free the marooned ship from the reef, and its crew and passengers were finally able to escape. Weeks after, the captain of the rescue ship was not so fortunate—he was beheaded by the islanders.

Because of their debilitated conditions, Jack and Charmian and two of their crew boarded a passenger boat headed for Australia so that they could seek treatment for their serious illnesses. Jack was confined to the hospital for five weeks and was still not fully recovered when he checked out.

Physically depleted, he told Charmian that he could not continue on their cruise. Charmian had savored the cruise and had worked alongside the men, always holding her own. Her dream adventure cut short, she "was wrecked and broken" for two days. They sold the Snark for a pittance.

Jack and Charmian left Australia on a tramp steamer in April 1909, and during their lengthy journey home, both recovered their health. By July they were back in California after an absence of twenty-seven months.

THE RANCH AND SUSTAINABLE FARMING

UPON THEIR RETURN JACK and Charmian's thoughts turned to improving their Beauty Ranch. Within a year they purchased a large parcel of additional land, expanding the ranch to more than a thousand acres.

Jack was not unacquainted with ranching, having spent eight years of his youth on ranches along the San Mateo coast and in Livermore, but it had not appealed to him then. Still, something elemental in it had lodged in his bones and emerged later into his consciousness for he was now devoted to the ranch. He considered soil the world's most valuable asset.

He read scores of agricultural journals and sought advice from Luther Burbank in nearby Santa Rosa. As in all things, he approached the management of the ranch with intensity, always putting the soil first: "I am that sort of farmer, who, after delving in all the books to satisfy his quest for economic wisdom, returns to the soil as the source and foundation of all economics."

He adopted sustainability as ranch policy, stating: "I am rebuilding worn-out hillside lands that were worked out and destroyed by our wasteful California pioneer farmers. I am not using commercial fertilizer. I believe the soil is our one indestructible asset, and by green manures, nitrogen-gathering cover crops, proper tillage and drainage, I am getting results . . ."

Jack conceived of a large family house to be built on the ranch in a style described by his architect as "American rustic." The redwood timbers, stone, and other materials were to be gathered from the surrounding land whenever possible. Jack named the rising family home "Wolf House."

He dreamed of the ranch as a self-sufficient community with housing for the workers and perhaps a school for the children. He began writing *The Valley of the Moon* with a back-to-the-land theme. Later, he said: "Among all my books, I think, *The Call of the Wild* is the most popular one, but *The Valley of the Moon* is [the] most ideal one to me."

THE SPARK

IN 1913, A YEAR that Jack called his "bad year," he finished *John Barleycorn*, his autobiographical novel of his struggles with alcohol. In August the nearly completed Wolf House burned down. The emotional pain its destruction caused him also manifested itself physically in his once-invulnerable body.

By 1915, it had become obvious that Jack's health was in steep decline. His kidneys and urinary system were failing, and his body was bloated. In the spring Jack and Charmian traveled to Hawaii, and Jack's health improved temporarily. He was unfailingly interested in discussing ranch and farming issues or the thrill of sea adventure but adamantly avoided discussing literature.

The following year Jack and Charmian traveled again to Hawaii for several months, returning to the Beauty Ranch in mid-summer. Jack's kidneys were now gravely affecting his health, and he suffered from uremic poisoning, dysentery, and insomnia.

On the night of November 21, as Jack was turning in, he startled Charmian by saying "Thank God, you're not afraid of anything." Those were his last words to her. He died the next day at just forty years old.

The *San Francisco Bulletin* headlined its full-page eulogy: "JACK LONDON IS DEAD! HE OF ALL MEN WAS SUPREMELY ALIVE!"

Charmian continued to live at the Beauty Ranch until her death in January, 1955. The ranch, the graves of Jack and Charmian, the ruins of Wolf House, and other structures and mementos are preserved at Jack London State Historic Park located near Glen Ellen. The grounds and lakes are beautiful, and visitors are generally free to walk around and hike the park's trails.

During his life Jack wrote fifty books and scores of articles and other works. His books and stories have been widely translated, and several have been adapted into movies. His legacy of work is particularly astounding in view of the numerous and varied adventures he squeezed into his short life.

We will close with Jack's own words spoken two months before he died. They express the credo by which he lived:

> I would rather be ashes than dust! I would rather that my spark should burn out in a brilliant blaze than it should be stifled by dry rot. I would rather be a superb meteor, every atom of me in magnificent glow, than a sleepy and permanent planet. The proper function of man is to live, not to exist. I shall not waste my days in trying to prolong them. I shall use my time.

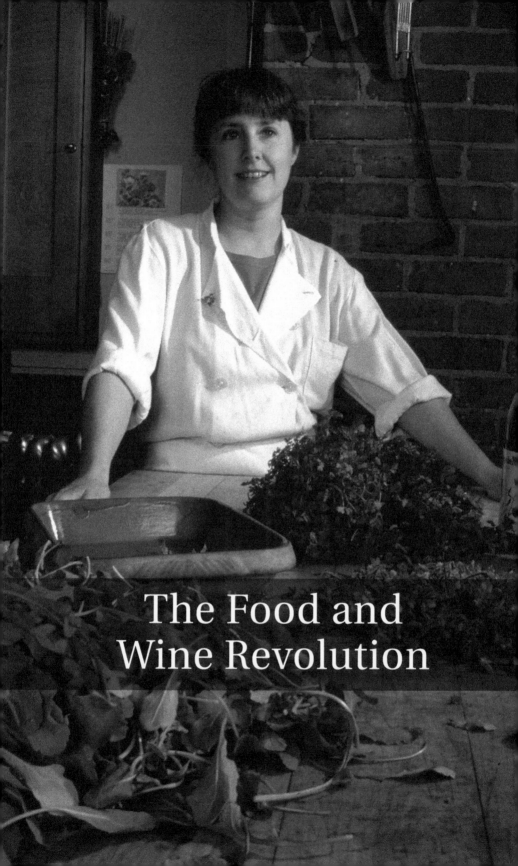

The Food and
Wine Revolution

THE FOOD AND WINE REVOLUTION

I N THE BEGINNING THERE was Alice Waters and the word "taste." Over time there would be far more people and far more words, and the revolution in food would encompass far more than just restaurants and cooking. It would engender deep cultural changes in farming, food markets, and consumer taste. It would require innovation and attentiveness to soil, climate, and season. But let's start with Alice.

When she opened Chez Panisse in Berkeley in 1971, it was not revolutionary except in one respect—it had a single daily dinner menu with no à la carte choices. Although the menu was usually created spontaneously, the ideas of "seasonal" and "local" were not yet a part of it. The focus was on taste, so much so that it was almost a mantra.

A new menu was posted daily because Alice wanted "the food to be alive and perfect every night." All that followed at the restaurant came from her devotion to taste, the demands of the single daily menu, and her open mind.

Alice was not usually the head chef. She was more like a hands-on coach who placed every person in the perfect role. Influenced strongly by her time spent in France, she wanted to make simple French country food, like roast chicken, or lamb with beans. In its first years Chez Panisse felt part homey, part Berkeley. The staff and customers resembled a large family seasoned with a splash of counterculture.

In the early 1970s, Alice traveled to France again and fell in love with mesclun, a mix of a variety of young salad greens. She brought some seeds back with her and planted them in her backyard garden so that Chez Panisse could serve mesclun in its salads. Alice used her backyard mesclun in the restaurant's salads for several years before Northern California farmers realized there was demand for it and began growing and supplying it.

Salads were important to Alice. In the late 1970s she was invited to New York City to cook a dish at an event featuring Playboy magazine's selection of the country's top twenty-five restaurants. Chez Panisse had been listed as number seven. Alice elected to prepare the restaurant's mesclun salad for her dish and took little lettuces just picked in California with her on the plane to New York.

At the event Alice was wore an antique maroon dress and was flanked by the other chefs, all men clad in dark suits. They were preparing elaborate haute cuisine dishes, and Alice was making a green salad. Amazingly her salad stood out from the surrounding fancy fare and was the big news the next day.

She felt she had been somewhat naïve about the event, but she was proud of the simplicity of what Chez Panisse was doing nightly. She wrote later: "I think if there's one thing I'm responsible for in this country, something that I can take a little credit for, it's the propagation of real salad in the United States."

By the mid-1970s seasonality had started to make its way on to the Chez Panisse menu. It began when a woman brought French breakfast radishes from her garden to the restaurant, and they were served fresh that day. Then people began bringing Meyer lemons and blackberries from their yards, which were incorporated into daily dishes. The restaurant was still buying most of its vegetables from Berkeley's Monterrey Market, which was attuned to freshness but did not carry great variety.

About that time a French friend of Alice's sent her a big box of slender green beans—called haricots verts in French—from Chino Ranch outside San Diego. Soon Chez Panisse began purchasing much of its produce from Chino Ranch. It was the start of a long-term relationship that has survived to the present as the exception to the restaurant's commitment to purchase locally.

Food is much more than cooking—it is about geography, agriculture, nature, and culture. The back-to-the-land movement played a large part. The movement had started in the late 1960s and accelerated into the 1970s, glorifying small farms, sustainable practices, and a healthy environment. In time the smaller farmers, many of whom had migrated back to the land, would constitute the foundation of the food revolution.

Chez Panisse's special menu for October 7, 1976 was somewhat prescient in focusing on local items. Entitled "Northern Regional California Dinner," it featured "Spenger's Tomales Bay Bluepoint oysters on ice; Big Sur Garrapata Creek smoked trout steamed over California bay leaves; Monterey Bay prawns sautéed with garlic, parsley, and butter; preserved California-grown geese from Sebastopol; Vella dry Monterey Jack cheese from Sonoma; Fresh caramelized figs, walnuts, almonds, and mountain pears from the San Francisco Farmers' Market." The restaurant wanted to source locally, but a reliable supply chain for local items was lacking.

Wine was still not a large part of the restaurant scene. In 1966 Robert Mondavi had announced his intention to make California wines that would compete with the best from France and bring a wine culture to America. He trained winemakers Mike Grgich and Warren Winiarski with that goal in mind. They in turn would figure prominently in the Paris Wine Tasting of 1976, a defining event for American wine.

THE PARIS TASTING

On May 24, 1976, just after 3 p.m., Steven Spurrier stood up in a room at the Paris InterContinental Hotel and asked the judges and the modest audience for their attention. He announced that he and Patricia Gallagher were holding the event to taste several interesting California wines and similar French ones to celebrate the two hundredth anniversary of American independence and France's aid to the American colonies during that time.

Spurrier was British and the owner of a highly regarded wine shop in Paris that sold quality French wines but none from California. With his assistant Patricia Gallagher, he also taught courses in wine tasting.

Gallagher and Spurrier had separately traveled to California and sampled some California wines. From that experience they selected six California cabernet sauvignons and six chardonnays to be included in the wine tasting. Spurrier also chose four French reds from Bordeaux and four whites from Burgundy that he considered premier wines that resembled the California wines in regard to aging.

He thought the famous Château Mouton Rothschild from Bordeaux would be the judge's top choice among the reds and that the Bâtard–Montrachet would place first among the whites.

The nine judges, all French, were well-respected wine experts and tasting veterans. The tasting was to be blind—that is, the wine would be poured from neutral bottles to exclude any indication of the name of the winery or country of origin.

Each judge was furnished with a scorecard and pencil, two empty wine glasses, a small roll to cleanse his or her palate between wines, and a champagne bucket in which to spit. Bottles of mineral water were also available.

The rules for the tasting were standard in France. Each judge was to grade up to twenty points on each of a wine's four elements: eye for color and clarity, nose, taste, and harmony among the sensations.

In the audience there was only one member of the press, George M. Taber from *Time* magazine. He later wrote the authoritative book on the tasting, The Judgment of Paris.

The waiters poured each of the judges a glass of Chablis to prepare their palates for the tasting. As usual the whites were poured first, their order determined randomly.

Taber, as the sole journalist, had been informed of the order of the pouring; the judges had not. He quickly realized from the comments the judges were making among themselves that they were often in error in distinguishing between the California and French wines. One judge even mistook France's famous Bâtard–Montrachet (the wine Spurrier had thought would place first among the whites) as clearly of California origin because it had no nose.

The judges gazed at each wine's color, sniffed, swirled the wine in their glasses, and sniffed again. They paused and took a sip letting the wine roll over their tongues and caress the inside of their mouths. After each tasting they marked their cards, recording their scores.

Spurrier had planned to wait until the conclusion of the entire event to announce the results. However, the preparation for the tasting of the reds took longer than expected, and he decided to fill the dead time by announcing the judges' determination for the whites.

Placing first was California's 1973 Chateau Montelena, crafted by winemaker Mike Grgich. It was followed by a French wine, and then two more California ones. Everyone was shocked that California whites had won first place and captured three of the first four places.

As the waiters began to pour the reds, Spurrier was confident the judges would have no trouble differentiating the French reds from the California ones. The French reds had unique tastes well known to the judges.

The room was pin-dropping quiet as Spurrier read the results of the cabernet tasting. Once more there was shock! California's Napa Valley had prevailed again. The 1973 Stag's Leap Wine Cellars Cabernet Sauvignon, crafted by Warren Winiarski, was the winner over France's famous 1970 Château Mouton Rothschild. The judges were stunned and dismayed.

Stag's Leap bested Château Mouton Rothschild by only a slim margin. Yet regardless of the margin of victory, a large chasm always exists between first and second place.

Spurrier and Gallagher walked out of the wine tasting together. They expressed their surprise and moved on to other topics, giving the event little more thought at the time. Indeed, the French press and the French wine establishment totally ignored the event.

But not for long. Taber's account of the tasting appeared in *Time* magazine's June 7, 1976, issue in the Modern Living section, positioned rather innocuously below the section's lead article. Still, Time had a readership then of twenty million, and news of the tasting spread quickly.

Newspapers all over the country trumpeted the California wine industry's victory over its French counterpart. The tasting stimulated a new American pride in domestic wines, and many who generally did not drink wine—or if they did, drank foreign wines—began drinking California wines.

In his autobiography *Harvests of Joy* Robert Mondavi stated: "The Paris tasting was an enormous event in the history of California wine making. It put us squarely on the world map of great wine-producing regions. I saw the impact everywhere I went."

At the time of the tasting, the 1973 Stag's Leap cabernet had a suggested retail price of $6.00. The next year Stag's Leap boosted it to $7.50—but the increase in wine's popularity in America was much greater.

After the tasting, wine became stylish. It changed its usual residence from jugs to attractive bottles. Restaurants adopted wine as an integral part of the dining experience. Wine shops proliferated, and supermarkets carried an expanded selection.

One measure of wine's upsurge in popularity is the huge increase in the number of wineries in Napa Valley: in the fall of 1968 there were 17 active Napa wineries—as of 2020 some 550.

There were many reasons for wine's emergence as a standard part of dining and life in America: a boom in European travel and exposure to its wine culture, a desire for something new, and a merger with the food revolution's emphasis on taste.

Yet, the perception of wine was markedly different after the Paris Tasting. Robert Parker, Jr., for many years widely considered the pre-eminent wine authority, perhaps stated it best: "The Paris Tasting destroyed the myth of French supremacy and marked the democratization of the wine world. It was a watershed in the history of wine."

After the tasting, wine joined food at the table, and they became partners in the revolution.

LOCAL, LOCAL, LOCAL

IN 1979 THE SAN Francisco Zen Center opened Green's, a vegetarian restaurant that broke new ground in the freshness and tastiness of its food. Its produce was generally supplied by the Zen Center's own Green Gulch Farm in Marin County. After visiting Green Gulch, Alice wanted her restaurant to have its own ready supply of fresh produce.

Chez Panisse initiated a concerted effort to source local seasonal food. Sibella Kraus, a line chef at the restaurant, was named its official "forager" tasked with finding and purchasing the best fresh ingredients from local sources.

With help from Chez Panisse and other notable restaurants, Sibella started the Farm-Restaurant Project in 1983 to create a permanent supply chain from local farms to local restaurants.

Early in the endeavor she called upon Warren Weber at Star Route Farms in Bolinas, the oldest certified organic farm in California. Weber was legendary in the organic farming movement, but Sibella was primarily interested in the quality of the produce, not its organic credentials. Chez Panisse's devotion was to taste and local sourcing, and it was not then focused on organic ingredients, as it would be later.

At the time Star Route, like other organic farms, was supplying health food stores but not restaurants. Star Route was worried that if it devoted a portion of its crops to the specialty produce desired by restaurants, the restaurants might later purchase it from less expensive suppliers, leaving Star Route with unsalable product. It and other producers soon resolved the problem with protective contracts.

The restaurants wanted arugula and mesclun so Weber bought and planted the seeds, expanding Star Route's offerings. As demand increased, Weber purchased greenhouses in the Coachella Valley so that Star Route could grow and supply seasonal produce all year.

The surging demand for local farm fresh produce and fruit began expanding beyond produce to other foods, including specialty cheese and meats.

Laura Chenel has a reputation for being the mother of goat cheese in this country, but she owes a large part of that reputation to Alice. Cheese had been made in California since soon after the gold rush, but the boom created by Chenel's goat cheese was unprecedented.

Born and raised in Sonoma County, Chenel started a small farm in Sebastopol during the back-to-the-land movement. She began with bees, chickens, a vegetable garden, fruit trees, and most importantly a couple of goats. She was passionate about her goats and began making cheese from their milk. Then, she tasted a slice of French goat cheese and her life expanded.

She began learning French and wrote to the French author of a book on making artisanal cheese. He invited her to France and arranged a brief apprenticeship for her with a cheese maker in a mountain village. Her enthusiasm carried her on to work at a second French farm.

After some time Chenel returned to the United States to give her new skills a try. She was making goat cheese daily when she met Alice Waters in 1979, a life-changing event. Alice put her fresh cheese on the Chez Panisse menu and soon the restaurant began to pick it up daily for the restaurant's signature salad.

Cheese shops and restaurants all over California followed Alice's lead and ordered Chenel's cheese. Wolfgang Puck used it on his pizza. Square One wrapped it in phyllo and baked it to serve with its salad. Others grilled it, wrapped it, or served it other ways. Goat cheese was ubiquitous in California restaurants and those throughout the country. To many it was the symbol of California cuisine.

In 1974 Bill Niman and journalist and activist Orville Schell opened a ranch in Bolinas raising pigs and soon beef cattle as well. They raised their animals on a natural diet and babied them. Sometimes the cows would frolic in the surf off Bolinas, and Niman would have to venture into the cold ocean to chase them back to land.

Niman-Schell was selling its beef and pork to markets, natural food stores, and other consumers but not restaurants. However, following a 1985 national news story about the company, Chez Panisse and other restaurants seeking local sources contacted Niman. Soon Niman-Schell beef occupied a place of honor, listed by name on the menus of Chez Panisse, Zuni Café, Square One, and Stars.

As the demand for fresh specialty and artisanal food surged, corporations and large-scale farmers jumped aboard the trend. Smaller producers capitalized on the shift in taste to "small is beautiful" and "local is freshest," selling their products at farmers' markets and directly to restaurants.

Farmers' markets burst on to the scene early in the 1980s and by the end of the decade were present in almost every community. Chefs could now purchase high quality local foods either straight from the farms or at farmers' markets.

By the end of the 1980s the new style of cooking and eating pioneered by Alice Waters had changed the offerings of supermarkets and the character of meals served at home across the country. There was a widespread devotion to freshness, local sources, seasonality, and sustainability. Whole Foods had entered the scene and the television air waves were filled with celebrity chefs revealing their secrets for making tasty meals.

Seasonality and its two cousins, buying local and freshness, are devoted to ripeness, the essence of taste in each vegetable and fruit. With ripeness as a guide, it is clear there are many more seasons than just four. The period of ripeness offered by each specific vegetable and fruit constitutes a season all by itself, one whose timing depends on topography, weather, soil and other factors. In fact, each variety of each vegetable and fruit has its own separate season of ripeness.

Alice emphasizes seasonality and buying local for reasons beyond taste. A devotion to seasonality encourages sustainability and diversity and supports local communities. It encourages health—that of the land and the area's inhabitants.

Many years ago, at a middle school in Berkeley, she began the Edible Schoolyard Project, a garden and kitchen program promoting sustainability, seasonality, and healthy local foods for the children's lunches. There are now some seven thousand similar programs throughout the world. Alice believes elementary school is the perfect time and place to teach children to value taste and health, and to support sustainability through a commitment to their local communities.

The food revolution is unique in that it shuns canned, frozen, and processed foods and the arc of technology which created them. It rejects industrial agriculture and the monoculture associated with fast food, which destroys the diversity, sustainability and regard for the land of local agriculture.

It hearkens back to a simpler time when the only foods available were local, fresh ingredients. It stresses taste over convenience and speed. It has embraced many ethnic foods—now an integral part of the diverse American food scene—and has made organic food virtually standard in many places.

The food revolution has created more direct and immediate relationships between the farmer and the market and between the consumer and food. Using taste as a guide, and devoted to the concepts of local, seasonal, and sustainable, it continues to forge a new eating culture in this country and a healthier relationship with food, the land, and the entire environment.

For the new culture and its many delightful meals, we can gratefully hold our glasses high to Alice.

A Historic Camping Trip

A HISTORIC CAMPING TRIP

IN 1903 PRESIDENT THEODORE Roosevelt was planning a spring tour of the western states and wanted very much to camp with John Muir in Yosemite, but he was informed that Muir would be out of the country.

Roosevelt wrote to Muir immediately with an offer he could not refuse: "I do not want anyone with me but you, and I want to drop politics absolutely for four days and just be out in the open with you."

Muir was generally a purist when it came to preservation, but he could also be a realist. Unable to resist the opportunity "to do some forest good in talking freely around the campfire" with the president, he postponed his other plans.

The intimacy and exchange of ideas between the two luminaries on their camping trip in May of 1903 led to the preservation of some of the nation's and California's most extraordinary natural sites. Those preservation efforts were accomplished only after some ingenious political moves, which have also resulted in preservation successes in our own times.

John Muir's rise to fame as a conservationist and nature writer began in the spring of 1869 when he walked from San Francisco for his first view of Yosemite. On the way Muir marveled at the untrammeled Central Valley as a "furred, rich sheet of golden compositae" pushing up against the luminous Sierra Nevada. He thought a better name for the Sierra would be "the Range of Light."

That summer Muir worked as a shepherd at Tuolumne Meadows in Yosemite's high country, and the following year he operated a sawmill in Yosemite Valley. He visited Hetch Hetchy for the first time in 1871 and spent the next several summers exploring the Sierra Nevada's glaciers and ascending various mountain summits, including Mt. Shasta.

In his first book, The Mountains of California, Muir wrote of climbing and perching atop a hundred-foot Douglas fir during an exhilarating storm, "free to take the wind into his pulses," sense the "wild exuberance of light and motion," and see the wind "about as visible as flowing water." Muir wrote of glaciers and meadows, of forests and bee pastures, and of his favorite bird the water ouzel or dipper, a frequenter of waterfalls. His acute and often lyrical descriptions of nature's wonders are unmatched.

In 1892 Muir co-founded the Sierra Club, and he served as its president for the rest of his life. His house was located in Martinez, California, but to most his real home has always been Yosemite.

Our brief account of Roosevelt begins on his darkest day, Valentine's Day of 1884, when first his mother and then his wife died—his wife just two days after giving birth to their first child. Devastated, Roosevelt wrote in his diary: "The light has gone out of my life."

He retreated to his ranch in the Dakota Territory and bought another ranch there, even further removed from civilization. He traveled and observed the destruction of forests and wildlife resulting from the nation's western expansion.

During the catastrophic Dakota winter of 1886–87, the bulk of his cattle died and his herd never recovered. That and the earlier loss of his wife and mother brought home to him the fragility of life in a very personal way. It helped hone his determination to preserve the country's unsurpassed natural resources, particularly in the West.

Roosevelt, while serving as the country's vice president, became president in 1901 when William McKinley was assassinated. On his western tour in 1903 he visited Yellowstone National Park and the Grand Canyon, which particularly captivated him. Then he headed to the West Coast and his longed-for camping trip with John Muir.

Upon entering Yosemite, Muir and Roosevelt rode directly to the Mariposa Grove of giant sequoias, which was outside the national park. "These are the big trees, Mr. Roosevelt," Muir said. Roosevelt responded that it was "the greatest forest site" he had ever seen and declared, "It is good to be with you, Mr. Muir."

That night they dined on fried chicken and beefsteak. Shortly after dinner the president said he was fatigued from his travels and retired to bed in the open air under the Grizzly Giant, the Mariposa Grove's largest tree.

They broke camp early the next morning with Roosevelt telling Ranger Charles Leidig to "outskirt and keep away from civilization." Later, after downing a cold lunch, the small party traveled through deep snow as they crossed Bridalveil Meadows and fought through high wind and snow up to Sentinel Dome and ultimately a campsite farther on.

Muir and Roosevelt's relationship really developed on the second night of the camping trip. After dinner they relaxed and talked around the campfire surrounded by darkness and five feet of snow near Glacier Point. They stared at the sparking fire and took in the vault of stars overhead. Suddenly Muir jumped up and yelled, "Watch this!" With that he snatched a flaming branch from the fire, stepped outside the firelight, and torched a dead pine tree on a nearby ledge above the valley.

As the fire shot skyward from the tree, Muir danced a joyous jig around the towering flames, his long shadow aping his movements. Roosevelt jumped up and joined in, yelling "Hurrah" repeatedly into the night. "That's a candle it took five hundred years to make," shouted Roosevelt. "Hurrah for Yosemite, Mr. Muir!"

They talked far into the night with Muir expounding his glacier theory for the creation of Yosemite Valley. They discussed the necessity of conserving of the nation's vast forests generally and the trees in Yosemite Valley specifically. Roosevelt spoke of his desire to create several national parks in the West, particularly one for the threatened Grand Canyon, which had so captured his passion.

By now Muir and Roosevelt were completely comfortable with each other, and they reinforced each other's views. According to Ranger Leidig, the only conversational difficulty was that each "wanted to do the talking." That night while it snowed five inches, they slept comfortably on a bed of boughs and ferns that Muir had prepared.

In the morning they traveled on horseback to Glacier Point for prearranged photographs and then to Little Yosemite Valley for lunch. A considerable crowd awaited the president at the top of Nevada Falls, and he requested that they be kept at a distance so he could continue with his desired "roughing trip."

As they were making their way down into Yosemite Valley for their third overnight campsite, Muir explained to President Roosevelt that he had an ulterior motive for the camping trip, some very specific requests for areas that desperately needed federal protection. Roosevelt had an agenda too. He hoped that this widely publicized camping trip with Muir would help him politically and also ease the way for his conservation aims. Their discussion would wait until that night.

They made camp on a grassy slope beyond the spray of Bridalveil Falls. The president took a quick nap, snoring so loudly that he could be heard even above the sound of the falls and the popping of the campfire. After dinner Muir and the President walked out into the meadow alone and talked well into the night.

Muir asked the president pointedly to incorporate abused Yosemite Valley and the Mariposa Grove of the huge sequoias, both owned by the State of California, into Yosemite National Park. He advocated passionately for federal ownership to halt the felling of timber in the valley that was occurring under state management. As Muir later boasted, "I stuffed him pretty well regarding the timber thieves." Separately, Muir requested the president to save Mt. Shasta.

Roosevelt was receptive to Muir's wishes, but he had his own wider preservation agenda that had been energized and broadened by his western loop. He particularly wanted to save the Grand Canyon from mining and other development and some archeological sites in Arizona and the Four Corners area from widespread plundering.

In all of these matters, Muir and the president were united. Muir later told a friend, "Camping with the president was a remarkable experience. I fairly fell in love with him." Their underlying differences regarding preservation were unspoken at the time but would surface later in the battle over Yosemite's Hetch Hetchy Valley, a controversy famous to this day.

Immediately after leaving Yosemite, the president telegrammed the secretary of the interior to prepare an order to expand the federal forest reserves to include Mt. Shasta.

Afterward he wrote Muir an appreciative letter: "I shall never forget our three camps; the first in the solemn temple of the giant sequoias; the next in the snowstorm among the silver firs near the brink of the cliff; and the third on the floor of the Yosemite, in the open valley, fronting the stupendous rocky mass of El Capitan, with the falls thundering in the distance on either hand."

In direct response to Muir's desire to save Mt. Shasta, Roosevelt enclosed his telegram requesting preparation of the order that would accomplish it immediately. It would take Roosevelt much longer to overcome the obstacles to his own preservation agenda and Muir's requests as to Yosemite.

In Sacramento shortly after departing Yosemite, Roosevelt gave a speech that reflected how much his camping experience with Muir had affected him and focused his thinking:

"Lying out at night under the giant sequoias had been like lying in a temple built by no hand of man, a temple grander than any human architect could by any possibility build. . . .it would be a shame to our civilization to let them disappear. . . . We are not building this country of ours for a day. It is to last through the ages."

After his election to a second term in 1904, Roosevelt was determined to push through the conservation legislation that he and Muir had discussed. He was interested primarily in protecting the Grand Canyon and expanding Yosemite National Park to include the valley and Mariposa Grove. Congressional resistance to these seemingly simple measures convinced Roosevelt that he needed a path around Congress to implement his preservation goals.

In 1906 Congress finally approved the expansion of Yosemite National Park, but it stymied the rest of Roosevelt's program, including protection of the Grand Canyon. In response to this congressional recalcitrance, Roosevelt hardened his resolve and intensified his search for a means to bypass Congress altogether.

One of Roosevelt's closest allies, Representative John Lacey, finally provided him with the magic wand he craved. In 1906 Lacey, who was interested in protecting Devils Tower near the Black Hills and certain archaeological sites in Arizona and the Four Corners area, pushed through legislation entitled "Act for the Preservation of American Antiquities."

The Antiquities Act gave the president the unilateral power to designate areas as national monuments without consulting Congress or obtaining its approval. Lacey had shepherded the act through Congress with little opposition because it seemed on its surface to apply only to the preservation of prehistoric and historic sites. But it contained two seemingly innocuous words that provided the much wider power that Roosevelt desired, for it applied also to sites of "scientific interest."

Soon after the passage of the Antiquities Act, Roosevelt used his power to preserve sites dear to Lacey's heart. Later he was requested to use his new power to prevent the destruction of an isolated canyon on Mt. Tamalpais that held Marin County's last surviving stand of virgin redwoods.

Roosevelt had become entranced with redwoods on his western tour. Before going to Yosemite, he had visited sites around Santa Cruz and Monterey and been particularly moved by the lofty redwoods. He asked for private time with them and declared that they ought to be preserved and "left unmarred for our children and our children's children and so on down the ages."

The redwoods in the canyon on Mt. Tam had stood sentinel when Columbus discovered America, had co-existed for centuries with the Bay Area's first inhabitants, and had survived the relentless lumbering that began with the gold rush. John Steinbeck fittingly called redwoods, "ambassadors from another time."

William Kent, a giant in the preservation of Marin County lands, had purchased Marin's isolated stand of redwoods in 1905 to save them from development. When his wife had objected to his borrowing funds to buy the land, Kent had famously replied, "If we lost all the money we have and saved those trees, it would be worthwhile, wouldn't it?"

But in early December of 1907 a new threat arose. A water company brought an eminent domain lawsuit to condemn the canyon of redwoods for use as a reservoir to serve Mill Valley's growing populace. Kent was counseled that the only possible savior for the redwoods was the recently enacted Antiquities Act.

On December 23, 1907, Kent wrote a letter offering the federal government his deed to the canyon of redwoods for designation as a national monument under the Antiquities Act. He asked that it be named Muir Woods in honor of John Muir. Kent had never met Muir, but he thought Muir's name carried the right message about the importance of preservation.

President Roosevelt acted quickly. On January 9, 1908 he declared Muir Woods a national monument, stating that it was "of extraordinary scientific interest." The correspondence between Roosevelt and Kent that followed provides some insight into the character of each.

On January 23,1908, Roosevelt wrote to Kent: "You have doubtless seen my proclamation of January 9th, instant, creating the monument. . . . I have a great admiration for John Muir; but . . . this is your gift and I should greatly like to name it Kent Monument if you will permit it."

Kent responded on January 30: "Your kind suggestion of a change of name is not one that I can accept. I have five good, husky boys. If these boys cannot keep the name of Kent alive, I am willing it should be forgotten."

Roosevelt wrote back on February 5: "By George! You are right. . . . Good for you, and for the five boys who are to keep the name of Kent alive! I have four who I hope will do the same thing by the name of Roosevelt."

Ironically, John Muir's connection with Muir Woods was in name only. He expressed his reaction to its being named after him in a February 6, 1908, letter to Kent:

> Seeing my name . . . was a surprise of the pleasantest kind. This is the best tree-lover's monument that could possibly be found in all the forests of the world. . . . Saving these woods from the axe & saw from the money-changers & water-changers . . . is in many ways the most notable service to God and man I've heard of since my forest wanderings began. . . . Immortal sequoia life to you.

The conservationist good works by the three men associated with Muir Woods would continue, but the alliance between them would blow apart over Yosemite's Hetch Hetchy Valley and the proposal to make it a reservoir to supply water to thirsty San Francisco.

Muir thought flooding Hetch Hetchy Valley a desecration of one of nature's exquisite creations and was outspoken and eloquent in his opposition. A staunch preservationist, he decried the permanent sacrifice of one of nature's wonders to meet seemingly short-term needs.

To Kent, by then a U.S. congressman from Marin, making Hetch Hetchy a reservoir to supply water to San Francisco was the best use of a natural resource for the people's benefit, and he supported it. Still, he persisted in other conservationist acts. In 1928, with almost his last breath, he donated the spectacular Steep Ravine as the initial land for Mt. Tamalpais State Park.

Roosevelt's position fell somewhat between Kent's broader concept of conservation as including certain practical uses and Muir's purity of purpose. Ultimately Roosevelt refused Muir's entreaties to prevent the flooding of Hetch Hetchy. Its loss was John Muir's worst preservation defeat.

Muir's writing on Yosemite, other wild lands, and the beauty to be found in nature have long been an inspiration to nature lovers and preservationists. He turned conservation into a crusade and is still regarded as one of its foremost spokesmen. He died in 1914.

Roosevelt accomplished more for conservation than any other president. During his presidency he created or enlarged 150 national forests and established eighteen national monuments, fifty-one bird reserves, five new national parks, and four wildlife preserves. Two days after declaring Muir Woods a national monument, he did the same to protect the Grand Canyon, which became a national park eleven years later.

In California he declared both Lassen Peak and Cinder Cone national monuments. They were combined in 1916, with additional land, into Lassen National Park. Roosevelt also declared Pinnacles a national monument—his decision clinched by its status as a favored roosting site for the California condor. Pinnacles became a national park in 2013.

In all, Roosevelt preserved 234 million acres, 10 percent of our nation's present landmass. He brought conservation into the mainstream.

The Antiquities Act, Roosevelt's magical instrument, is still used effectively for preservation to this day. In 2000 President Bill Clinton used it to establish Sequoia National Monument, containing and protecting thirty-two separate groves of giant sequoias.

During the last days of his presidency, President Barack Obama, in the face of a hostile Congress and an adverse successor, created a new Bears Ears National Monument in Utah and designated six new coastal California areas as part of the existing California Coastal National Monument.

Muir Woods National Monument offers a ready and powerful perspective on time and preservation. Its redwoods have existed for centuries. Unprotected, they would have been cut down in days. Saved, they can take your breath away in a second.

Now imagine yourself in Yosemite on that famous camping trip in conversation with Muir and Roosevelt. Listen attentively as they discuss the Earth's natural communities, magnificent landscapes, and wildlife. The results of their historic meeting continue to reverberate into the present.

Still, the future is up to us. We must decide how much of our landscape, wildlife, and plant world will remain for our children and their children. Preserving much and restoring what we can is probably the most generous gift that we can give them. Then they can decide the future of the planet for themselves.

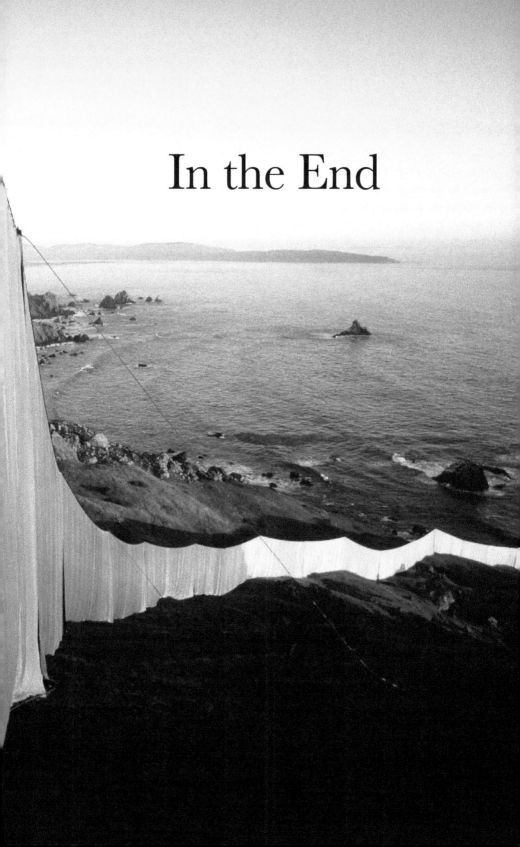

In the End

IN THE END

The most startling, most audacious statement ever made on California land was Christo's *Running Fence*. Its rippling white nylon stood eighteen feet tall. It strode across ridges, dipped into draws, and explored the land's wrinkled, uneven skin for more than twenty-four miles before plunging into the ocean off Marin County's coast. The fence's calling card was bravado, its stretch seemed infinite, it drew attention to the particular.

Running Fence originated in the mind of Christo but would have died there without the support, skill, and energy of his dynamic wife, Jeanne-Claude. They completed the astounding project in September of 1976 and removed it, as planned, two weeks later. Still, it has never disappeared from the minds and memories of its participants and viewers.

Everything about the fence trespassed the boundaries of reality. It was monumental in scope and unlike anything that had existed previously. Other monumental works, such as the Great Wall of China or the Egyptian Pyramids, were massive, lasted untold generations, and were constructed by tyrants on the backs of slaves or forced laborers.

Running Fence was light and airy, ephemeral like a blooming flower, and democratic in its reliance on fifty-nine ranch and farm families whose land it traversed and on the diverse paid laborers who built it. The ancient monuments are made of stone and are inert. Christo's fence was made of light fabric that seemed alive as it rippled, billowed, and ran before the wind. The only resemblance between the ancient monuments and the fence was the astonishment they created.

Christo made the initial drawings for *Running Fence* in late 1972. Early the next year he and Jeanne-Claude drove six-thousand miles up and down the California and Oregon coasts searching for a suitable place to showcase it. As a starting point they were looking for a spot for the fence to plunge into or emerge from the ocean, depending on your viewpoint. In addition they needed interior land with rolling hills, few trees, and roads from which to view the fence's expanse.

Christo ultimately selected a stretch of land beginning just east of Highway 101 outside Petaluma and traversing interior Sonoma County to coastal Marin and the Pacific Ocean off its far northern shore. The fence spanned Sonoma's dry, creased hills, avoiding the few natural trees gathered deep in the creases on the promise of water. On the coast, it dove into the ocean's curling breakers as they crashed and foamed below the bluffs. The white fence's taper from the bluffs into the ocean transformed at sunset into various shades of orange: peach to apricot to persimmon to fire.

Running Fence was not created by inspiration alone; it took persistence and patience. In 1974 Christo and Jeanne-Claude began meeting and befriending the ranchers and farmers whose land underlay the planned path of the fence. At first blush, ranchers and farmers might seem unlikely to support a huge visionary art project invading their land. Yet once they understood it, they became the fence's staunchest advocates.

Overcoming the obstacles presented by fifteen governmental agencies—most prominently the boards of supervisors of Sonoma and Marin counties and the California Coastal Commission—proved much more difficult. To make matters worse, a group of citizens formed the Committee to Stop the Fence, which then brought several lawsuits opposing it.

If the ranch owners were willing to have the fence run through their land, why were the various bureaucracies so reluctant to approve it, and why were some citizens so determined to defeat it?

The naysayers claimed that even though the project involved no public expenditure of funds, it was a materialistic, money-making project solely for the benefit of Christo and Jeanne-Claude and was simply a vast ego trip. Others argued that since the fence was temporary, it could not be art and was a waste of time and resources.

A farmer's wife spoke at one hearing and rebutted the last objection with a simple example: "Some of the meals I prepare aren't much. But sometimes I go to a lot of work to prepare a meal that I think is 'art.' It's a masterpiece. And what happens to it? It gets eaten up and disappears."

Underlying the various negative arguments was a bedrock resistance to change, an inherent opposition to something so dramatically new. The opponents refused to see the fence's imaginative, expansive power and preferred the straitjacket of inertia. Still whatever the rationales they offered, the naysayers could point to no harm that the fence would cause.

Christo applied to Marin County for the required permits in late 1974. Once acquainted with the fence, the Marin supervisors were receptive to it, and in early 1975 they approved it.

Sonoma was a different story. It took virtually all of 1975 to obtain the approval from that county's board, which finally gave it in a cliffhanger vote of 3–2.

The California Coastal Commission was the last obstacle, and it refused to issue a permit allowing the fence to cross the coast and make its tapering dive into the ocean. The California attorney general issued a warning threatening enforcement against any violation of the Coastal Commission's prohibition.

Christo, adamant that the fence run into the ocean, defied the Coastal Commission's ban. On September 3, 1976, he summoned a helicopter to bring in, under cover of a thick fog, the eleven steel support poles for the fence's descent into the ocean. A specially trained construction crew grabbed the poles from the hovering helicopter and planted them in a line from the bluff to the ocean floor.

The next day, the start of the extended Labor Day weekend, Christo ordered a barge anchored offshore. A cable was extended from the barge to the support poles descending into the ocean. In the darkening dusk, workers attached the last hundred yards of fabric to the cable slanting into the ocean. The final panel was hung under a full moon, the white fabric a specter casting its shadow over the undulating ocean waters.

Once the Labor Day weekend was over, the California Attorney General and the Committee to Stop the Running Fence asked Marin Superior Court Judge David Menary, on the basis of the violation, to issue a temporary restraining order stopping the erection of the remaining fence. Judge Menary refused to do so.

The fence was finally completed on September 10, and the crowds adored it. No one had ever seen anything like it. It evoked overwhelming emotions of wonder and awe.

As promised, Christo began removal of the fence on September 21. Two days later the Coastal Commission voted 7–1 to prohibit the fence in the coastal zone—even though it had already been removed. Furious and seeking revenge, the Coastal Commission pressed the attorney general to file a lawsuit for damages. Christo ultimately paid a compromise sum, a small price to pay for the realization of his dream and the public's great enjoyment. His take: "[It] is more important I cheat the law than I cheat my art."

Running Fence had many gaps to allow free movement through it. Even where there was no gap, it was not a barrier to keep things out but a way to bring them all together. The fence accentuated the landscape in new ways and stimulated people to delight in a fresh perception of their environment, rather than continue to be numbed to it by habit. People who had previously taken the landscape for granted now examined it closely with attentiveness and appreciation.

In some ways the fence was similar to the Golden Gate Bridge. Both joined water and land and animated the surrounding panorama. Each in its own way gathered within it the primal elements of sky, sun, earth, water and weather.

Running Fence probed the contours of its landscape. It yanked the dry, brown, grazed hills and pasture lands from anonymity. Its coin was audacity—one that Christo had used throughout his life.

He was born Christo Javacheff in Bulgaria in 1935. He left for communist Czechoslovakia in 1956 and escaped the Iron Curtain in 1957.

He met Jeanne-Claude the next year in Paris, and three years later they began working together on their bold projects. Their most famous early work was the *Wall of Oil Barrels—The Iron Curtain*. Constructed in 1962, it consisted of a high barricade of old, often rusty oil barrels that completely blocked a Paris street and all traffic. Some perceived it as a protest against the Berlin Wall. Others thought it suggested the divisions in French society. A few thought it symbolized consumerism's effect on the environment. Whatever its meaning, it was provocative.

Christo and Jeanne-Claude moved to New York in 1964 with their son, Cyril, and settled in a lower Manhattan building where they lived until their deaths, Jeanne-Claude's in 2009 and Christo's in 2020. Throughout their career, Christo and Jeanne-Claude earned international acclaim for their many immense and novel projects.

Just as *Running Fence* turned viewers' attention to the landscape, it is to the land that we must return. Several stories in this book have celebrated the land, its singularity, and the need for its preservation.

The landscape's magnificence is a gift, and we have preserved much of it. People save what they love and then love what they have saved. With the spread of urban centers and the accelerating sprawl of suburbia, the enduring beauty and accessibility of the remaining open lands is particularly special.

As Christo's *Running Fence* reminds us, we must hold and keep dear in our minds the unique essence of our lands. For in the end, "One generation passes away, and another generation comes, but the earth abides forever."

—PRINCIPAL SOURCES—

PRINCIPAL SOURCES

THE SOURCES LISTED BELOW were the most helpful but rarely the only sources for the stories. The origins of the quotes of John Steinbeck and Jack London are included separately following the sources for their stories.

A NEW REALM OF WONDER

My principal source for this story, as mentioned in the note at the end of the story proper, was Richard Preston's excellent book, *The Wild Trees* (2007).

I also consulted and used *The Last Redwoods and the Parkland of Redwood Creek*, by François Leydet (1969), *From the Redwood Forest Ancient Trees and the Bottom Line: A Headwaters Journey* by Joan Dunning (1998) and the article, "Issues and Impacts of Redwood National Park Expansion" by James K. Agee, published in *Environmental Management*, vol. 4, no. 5, pp 407–23 (1980), which I accessed online.

A MESSENGER FROM THE PAST

I relied extensively on two books, the first of which contains numerous documentary accounts:

Ishi the Last Yahi: A Documentary History edited by Robert F. Heizer and Theodora Kroeber (1979) includes multiple articles and accounts by each Saxton Pope, Al Kroeber, and T.T. Waterman, contemporary newspaper stories, reminiscences, anthropological accounts, and various other articles and extracts. I read some of the extracted historical accounts in full and can confirm that the extracts capture the relevant information.

Ishi in Two Worlds: A Biography of the Last Wild Indian in America by Theodora Kroeber (reprinted in 1961) is a fine biography that incorporates information from the specific documentary accounts and transforms it and other information about Ishi into a smooth and readable narrative flow.

SAVING THE CONDOR

I relied primarily on three books: John Moir's *Return of the Condor: The Race to Save Our Largest Bird from Extinction* (2006); John Nielsen's *Condor to the Brink and Back: The Life and Times of One Giant Bird* (2006); and Noel Snyder and Helen Snyder's *The California Condor: A Saga of Natural History & Conservation* (2000). This last book sets forth and explains well the several scientific issues confronting the recovery efforts.

I also consulted *The California Condor* by Carl B. Koford (1953).

THE TRUE PRIZE

My principal source, other than Steinbeck's own writing, is the superb biography of Steinbeck, Jackson J. Benson's *John Steinbeck, Writer*, previously published as *The True Adventures of John Steinbeck, Writer* (1984). I read it in the Penguin Books paperback edition published in 1990 (This is the edition I refer to below as *John Steinbeck, Writer*).

Steinbeck's own journal, *Working Days: The Journals of The Grapes of Wrath* published in 1989, long after his death, was an excellent source. I read it in the Penguin Paperback edition published by Heyday in 1990 (This is the edition I refer to below as *Working Days*). It contains an excellent introduction with notes by Robert DeMott.

Another fine source was *Steinbeck, A Life in Letters* (which I refer to below as *Letters*), edited by Elaine Steinbeck and Robert Wallsten (1975) and reissued by Penguin Books in 1989. Steinbeck was such a prolific correspondent that the editors were faced with the difficult task of paring the selection significantly, and as indicated below a few of the letters quoted are not included in *Letters*.

Steinbeck's seven articles on the migrants, published in the *San Francisco News* on consecutive days from October 5 to October 12, 1936 were republished in 2011 by Heyday in a thin paperback entitled *The Harvest Gypsies: On the Road to the Grapes of Wrath* (which I refer to below as *The Harvest Gypsies*).

The seven articles, plus Steinbeck's 1938 follow up article, "Starvation Under the Orange Trees," are contained in Steinbeck's *America and Americans and Selected Nonfiction*, edited by Susan Shillinglaw and Jackson J. Benson (1966) and republished by Viking Penguin in 2002.

I read or reread several books by Steinbeck before writing the story, but cite below only those quoted. The most important was, of course, *The Grapes of Wrath* (1939). Because it has been republished in countless editions, I give chapter numbers rather than page numbers for the quotes.

Another Steinbeck book quoted is *Sea of Cortez: A Leisurely Journal of Travel and Research* (1941), republished in paperback by Penguin in 2009 (This is the edition I refer to below as "*Sea of Cortez*"). *Journal of a Novel: The East of Eden Letters* (1969) is quoted once.

Quotes:

"Horses like her and dogs...": Letter to A. Grove Day, [December] 1929, in *Letters*.

"We pooled our troubles...": John Steinbeck's, "The Depression: A Primer on the 30s," *Esquire*, June 1960, pp. 86–87, quoted in *John Steinbeck, Writer*, p. 179.

"Nothing will ever stop me!": Martin Bidwell, "John Steinbeck: An Impression," *Prairie Schooner*, Spring 1938, pp. 12–14, quoted in *John Steinbeck, Writer*, p. 284.

"He admired anyone who...": *Journal of a Novel: The "East of Eden" Letters* (1969), p. 103 and contained in *Working Days*, Notes, part II to entry #16, p. 140.

"and Tom Collins trotted back and forth": John Steinbeck, "Forward" to *Bringing in the Sheaves*, by Thomas A. Collins, an unpublished novel manuscript, since published in *Journal of Modern Literature 2* (April 1976) (hereafter referred to as "Collins"), pp. 211–13, and quoted in *John Steinbeck, Writer*, p. 339.

"tired beyond sleepiness. . . ": Steinbeck's "Forward" to Collins, pp. 211–13, and quoted in *John Steinbeck, Writer*, p. 339.

"I just returned yesterday. . . ": Letter to literary agents in late September, 1936 quoted in *John Steinbeck, Writer*, p. 348 (not in *Letters*).

"the labor situation is so tense. . . ": Letter to George Albee, approximately late September 1936, in *Letters*.

"At the season of the year. . . ": *The Harvest Gypsies*, p. 19.

"Here, in the faces. . . ": *The Harvest Gypsies*, p. 27.

"There are about five thousand families. . . ": Letter to Elizabeth Otis, February 1938, in *Letters*.

"For forty-eight hours, and without food or sleep. . . ": Collins, pp. 221-224, quoted in *John Steinbeck, Writer*, p. 369.

"found John lying on his back. . . ": Collins, pp. 221–24, quoted in *John Steinbeck, Writer*, p. 369.

"It is bad because it is not honest. . . ": Letter to Elizabeth Otis, end of May 1938, quoted in *John Steinbeck, Writer*, p. 368 (not in *Letters*).

"Begin the detailed description. . . ": *Working Days*, entry #17, June 17, 1938, p. 29.

"Make the people live.": *Working Days*, entry #30, July 6, 1938, pp. 38–39.

"For the first time. . . ": *Working Days*, entry #12, June 11, 1938, p. 26.

"If only I could do this book. . . ": *Working Days*, entry #18, June 18, 1938, p. 29.

"But I am assailed. . . ": *Working Days*, entry #18, June 18, 1938, pp. 29–30.

"coroners fill in the [death] certificates. . . ": *The Grapes of Wrath*, chapter 25.

"in the eyes of the hungry. . . ": *The Grapes of Wrath*, chapter 25.

"I am sorry but I cannot change that ending. . . .": Letter to Pascal Covici, January 16, 1939, in *Letters.*

"I have never believed *The Grapes of Wrath* was exaggerated.": *Letters*, citing *New York Times* of April 3, 1940.

"May I thank you for your kind words.": Letter to Mrs. Franklin D. Roosevelt, April 24, 1940, in *Letters.*

"a nightmare all in all": Letter to Elizabeth Otis, October 1939, in *Letters.*

"the crash within myself": *Working Days*, entry #106, January 4, 1940, p. 110.

"It is one year less ten days. . . ": *Working Days*, entry #101, October 16, 1939, pp. 105–107.

"The loneliness and discouragement. . . ": Letter to Carlton (Dook) A. Sheffield, October 15, 1940, in *Letters.*

"I am working as hard. . . ": Letter to Pascal Covici, June 19, 1941, in *Letters.*

"relationship of animal to animal": *Sea of Cortez*, p. 216.

"that man is related to the whole thing. . . ": *Sea of Cortez*, p. 217.

"the tide pool to the stars. . . ": *Sea of Cortez*, p. 217.

"What it boils down to is. . . ": Letter to Pascal Covici, January 28, 1963, quoted in *John Steinbeck, Writer*, p. 923 (not in *Letters*).

"thought and feeling": *Working Days*, Entry #12, p. 26.

"and I'm desperately tired": Letter to Elizabeth Otis, September 10, 1938, in *Letters.*

BILL GRAHAM AND THE BIRTH OF THE SIXTIES

My principal written sources were *Bill Graham Presents: My Life Inside Rock and Out* by Bill Graham and Robert Greenfield (1990 and republished in 2004) and *Live at the Fillmore East and West: Getting Backstage and Personal with Rock's Greatest Legends* by John Glatt (2015). I also consulted *Summer of Love* by Joel Selvin (1994).

My source for the account of the rock festival on Mount Tamalpais is an article in *Rolling Stone* by Jason Newman dated June 1, 2014 entitled "The Untold Story of the First U.S. Rock Festival: The Fantasy Fair & Magic Mount Music Fest." I accessed it online.

I lived in or near San Francisco at the time, and some of my own experiences are reflected in the story.

THE PRISON ESCAPE ARTIST

I used several sources, but relied generally on David Grann's article, "The Old Man and the Gun" in *The New Yorker*, January 27, 2003, which I accessed online.

In connection with the escape from San Quentin, I interviewed Richard (Dick) Nelson regarding his actions and discoveries regarding the escape and other details of which he had contemporaneous knowledge.

I also used several contemporary newspaper articles describing the escape, the recaptures, and the trials, including, but not limited, to those at UPI.com from October 8, 1981 regarding Tucker's Boston capture at SFgate.com from April 28, 1999 about events after his Florida capture; historical recapitulations published on TCPalm.com on December 10, 2018; and a summation at LAtimes.com July 27,1999. I also consulted Edmond McGill's commentary in the November 28, 2018 *Marin Independent Journal* under "Marin Voice." All of these were accessed online.

The recollections of Tucker's daughter, Gaile, are from an article at Mirror.co.uk published on December 7, 2018, including her account of picking him up at the Miami airport in his disguise.

THE CALL OF THE WILD

I read many of Jack's stories and several of his books, including those cited in the quotes section, but not otherwise referenced below. His various short stories are contained in several books, including editions of his complete short stories.

I used Earle Labor's excellent biography, *Jack London: An American Life* (2014) for its overview and as my principal general source. Daniel Dyer's *Jack London: A Biography* (1997) was also useful.

I recommend two excellent books that contain fine and varied selections of Jack London's writings:

The Portable Jack London, edited by Earle Labor (1994) contains several of Jack's short stories, *The Call of the Wild*, a variety of his letters, and some nonfiction. The nonfiction includes autobiographical accounts presented in his essays, "What Life Means to Me," "How I Became a Socialist," and "Getting into Print," and in his letter to Houghton, Mifflin & Co. dated January 31, 1900. I used information and/or quotes from them all.

Jack London's Tales of Adventure, edited by Irving Shephard (1956) contains several short stories, selections from *The Cruise of the Snark* and various other books, and some nonfiction pieces, including "Through the Rapids on the Way to the Klondike" and "Dawson to the Sea" that are otherwise difficult to obtain.

I read and relied on Jack's letters contained in the three volume set, *The Letters of Jack London* (hereafter "*Letters*"), edited by Earle Labor, Robert C. Leitz, III, and I. Milo Shepard (1988).

Jack's autobiographical memoir, *John Barleycorn* (1913), is his own account of his problems with alcoholism, but also contains interesting information about other parts of his life.

My principal source on Jack's experiences in the Klondike was *Jack London's Klondike Adventure* by Mike Wilson (1995). Jack's own nonfiction accounts, "Through the Rapids on the Way to the Klondike" and "Dawson to the Sea," are the best sources for the time periods and experiences they cover and are contained in *Jack London's Tales of Adventure*. I also read *Jack London and the Klondike: The Genesis of an American Writer* by Franklin Walker (1966).

"The Gold Hunters of the North" is contained in *Revolution and Other Essays* by Jack London (1910 and reprinted in 2010) and was the source for the quotes about the Klondike truth stretching farther than the lies.

For Jack's cruise to the South Seas, I relied primarily on three sources: *Jack London in the South Seas* by A. Grove Day (1971), *Jack London: An American Life*, and Jack's own *The Cruise of the Snark*. I also quoted from his short story, "The Terrible Solomons." For many photos of Jack and the persons and places important to him and an accompanying, interesting account of his life, see A Pictorial Biography of Jack London by Russ Kingman (1979).

QUOTES

"I had no childhood. . . .": Letter to Mabel Applegarth, November 30, 1898, in *Letters*; also in *The Portable Jack London*.

"I was up and at work. . . ": Same as above.

"Hungry! Hungry! Hungry!. . . ": Same as above.

"wanted to be where the winds of adventure blew. . . .": *John Barleycorn*, chapter 7.

"The men in stripes. . . ": Same as above.

"glorious company of free souls": Same as above.

"the smack and slap of the spirit of revolt. . . ": Same as above.

"learning a trade could go hang. . . .": *John Barleycorn*, chapter 20.

"I became a tramp. . . ": "Road-Kids and Gay-Cats," in *The Road*

"throw his feet": "Confession," in *The Road*

"living hell": "The Pen," in *The Road*

"I had been born in the working class. . . ": "What Life Means to Me," in *The Portable Jack London*.

"I saw the picture of the Social Pit. . . ": "How I became a Socialist," in *The Portable Jack London*.

"to sell no more muscle. . . ": "What Life Means to Me," in *The Portable Jack London*.

"I read mornings, afternoons, and nights. . . .": *John Barleycorn*, chapter 5.

"work-beast": *John Barleycorn*, chapter 7.

"would have given a year's income. . . ": *Smoke Bellew*, chapter 1.

"Men broke their hearts. . . ": the story "Like Argus of the Ancient Times."

"rimrock to rimrock": *Jack London's Klondike Adventure*, p. 59; *Jack London & the Klondike*, p. 103.

"islands were silent and white. . . .": "A Day's Lodging."

"could not stretch the truth. . . ": "Gold Hunters of the North."

"but the truth could continue. . . ": "Gold Hunters of the North."

"White Silence": "The White Silence."

"home-made, weak-kneed and leaky": "From Dawson to the Sea."

"dreary, desolate Dawson": Same as above.

"overhanging forest, the smell of the land. . . ": Same as above.

"one gang holding up the edge. . . ": Quoting John Thorson in *Jack London's Klondike Adventure*, p. 115.

"almost entirely crippled me. . . ": Jack's diary quoted in *Jack London's Klondike Adventure*, p. 116 and *A Pictorial Biography*, p. 82.

"These few raw potatoes. . . ": Same as above.

"Leave St. Michaels. . . ": Jack's diary quoted in *Jack London's Klondike Adventure*, p. 124.

"It was in the Klondike that I found myself. . . .": "Through the Rapids on the Way to the Klondike."

"About the loneliest Christmas. . . ": Letter to Mabel Applegarth, Christmas morning, 1898, in *Letters*.

"I have never been so hard up. . . ": Letter to Edward Applegarth, Dec. 31, 1898, in *Letters*.

"he could cut down two-halves. . . ": "Getting into Print," in *The Portable Jack London*.

"He saved my literary life. . . ": Jack's introduction to *The Red-Hot Dollar and Other Stories from the Black Cat* (1911) by Herman Daniel Umbstaetter, quoted in *Jack London: An American Life*, chapter 10.

"I am afraid I always was an extremist.": *John Barleycorn*, chapter 16.

"A strong will can accomplish anything. . . .": Letter to Cloudsley Johns, March 30, 1899, in *Letters*.

"More money means more life. . . ": Letter to Cloudsley Johns, March 1, 1900, in *Letters*.

"great, great love": Letter to Charmian, August 14, 1903, in Earle Labor's private collection and quoted in *Jack London: An American Life*, chapter 15.

"I shall love you forever and forever.": Letter to Charmian, September 30, 1903, in *Letters*; also in *The Portable Jack London*.

"but it got away from me": Letter to George P. Brett, March 10, 1903, in *Letters*; also in *The Portable Jack London*.

"I don't seem to care for anything. . . ": In Charmian London's *The Book of Jack London*, volume 2, p 31 and quoted from *Jack London: an American Life*, chapter 17.

"the most beautiful, primitive land. . . ": Letter to George P. Brett, June 7, 1905, in *Letters*.

"Part of the process of recovering. . . ": *John Barleycorn*, chapter 30.

"We expect lots of action. . . ": Letter to Bailey Millard, February 18, 1906, in *Letters*.

"If I were a king. . . ": *The Cruise of the Snark*, chapter 15.

"that fever and dysentery. . . ": "The Terrible Solomons."

"a hearty appetite for human flesh. . . ": Same as above.

"was wrecked and broken": *The Cruise of the Snark*, last page.

"I am that sort of farmer. . . ": Letter to Geddes Smith, October 31, 1916, in *Letters*.

"I am rebuilding. . . ": Same as above.

"Among all my books. . . ": Third party interview of Jack, quoted in *Jack London: An American Life*, chapter 24.

"bad year": In Charmian London's *The Book of Jack London*, Volume 2, pp. 252-263 and quoted from *Jack London, An American Life*, chapter 25.

"I would rather be ashes than dust!. . . " Quoted in the Introduction to *Jack London's Tales of Adventure*, edited by Irving Shephard (1956). The words were reportedly spoken by Jack approximately two months before his death and were quoted by Ernest J. Hopkins in the *San Francisco Bulletin* of December 2, 1916.

THE FOOD AND WINE REVOLUTION

My principal sources on food were Alice Waters's memoir, *Coming to My Senses: The Making of a Counterculture Cook* (2017) and *Inside the California Food Revolution: Thirty Years that Changed Our Culinary Consciousness* by Joyce Goldstein, the chef and owner of the restaurant Square One in San Francisco, published in 2013.

I relied also on *We Are What We Eat: A Slow Food Manifesto* by Alice Waters (2021).

As to wine, I relied very heavily on *The Judgment of Paris: California vs. France and the Historic 1976 Paris Tasting That Revolutionized Wine* by George M. Taber (2005)

A HISTORIC CAMPING TRIP

I RELIED PRIMARILY ON *Wilderness Warrior: Theodore Roosevelt and the Crusade for America by Douglas Brinkley* (2009) and an accompanying ranger's account of the camping trip, "Charlie Leidig's Report of President Roosevelt's Visit in May, 1903" accessed online. To a lesser extent, I relied on *The Rise of Theodore Roosevelt* by Edmund Morris (1980).

My main source as to John Muir was *A Passion for Nature: The Life of John Muir* by Donald Worster (2008)

The excerpted nature quotes from John Muir's writing are from his first book, *The Mountains of California* (1894).

The most complete and detailed account of the preservation of Muir Woods is *The Historic Resources Study for Muir Woods National Monument* by John Auwaerter and John F. Sears (2006), which I accessed online.

IN THE END

My principal sources were two excellent books: *Christo: Running Fence: Sonoma and Marin Counties, California 1972-76*, edited by

Edith Pavese (1978) and *Christo and Jeanne-Claude: Remembering the Running Fence*, published under the auspices of the Smithsonian American Art Museum (2010).

I also found helpful and used *The Running Fence Project—Christo* with text by Werner Spies (Revised edition 1980) and *Christo and Jeanne-Claude: A Biography* by Bert Chernow (2002).

PHOTO CREDITS

1. Coast Redwoods in Northern California; Photo by Thomas Morris/Shutterstock.com.

2. Ishi shooting bow on Deer Creek, Tehama County, California; copyright © and courtesy of the Phoebe A. Hearst Museum of Anthropology and the Regents of the University of California, photograph by Saxton Temple Pope, Museum number 15-5823.

3. California condor at Pinnacles National Park; Photo by David Cahoun/Shutterstock.com.

4. John Steinbeck; Photo by Philippe Halsman/Magnum Photos.

5. Bill Graham, 1969; Photo by John Brenneis/The Chronicle Collection/Getty Images.

6. San Quentin State Penitentiary; Photo by Julie Vader/Shutterstock.com.

7. Jack and Charmian London in native clothes aboard the Snark in the South Seas; courtesy of The Huntington Library, San Marino, California, Jack London papers, mssJLP 1-782.

8. Alice Waters in the kitchen of Chez Panisse in Berkeley; Photo by Roger Ressmeyer/CORBIS/VCG via Getty Images.

9. John Muir and President Theodore Roosevelt in Yosemite; courtesy of Google Images commons.

10. *Running Fence* by Christo; Photo by Wolfgang Volz/laif/Redux

—ACKNOWLEDGMENTS—

ACKNOWLEDGMENTS

I can never thank enough people for their contributions to the book. Some have contributed recently, and others have made contributions that have been deeply ingrained in me for much of my life. To all I am deeply appreciative.

The seed for this book was planted by Carol Aquaviva, librarian and digital archivist at the Anne T. Kent California Room at the Marin County Civic Center Library. She suggested I write a story about the Rub-a-dub-dub escape from San Quentin. I expanded on that incident to create a story and then wrote this book.

In connection with the story, Carol encouraged me to call Jeff Creamer. He suggested I call Richard (Dick) Nelson, who spent many years working in different positions at San Quentin. Dick had contemporaneous knowledge of the escape, and related his personal knowledge to me over the telephone. He was a great help.

Laurie Thompson, Kent California Room librarian also encouraged me and had suggestions. She has recently retired and will be missed greatly.

Linda Giacomini told me about some personal social time she and her late husband, Gary Giacomini had spent with Christo and Jean-Claude and lent me several books that Christo had given them.

My early readers, in addition to my wife Mary, have been Buz Johanson, Maxene Kotin, and my brothers, John Holden and Paul Holden. Each gave me candid and excellent advice from their own perspectives. Kramer Herzog and Jay Rynbrandt each read a story and contributed their insights.

I greatly appreciate the invaluable guidance regarding the book that I received from Luisa Smith and E.H. Mann.

Hilary Roberts was a copy editor for several years at Penguin

Books and now, on her own, continues to render such services for Penguin Random House. She copyedited my grammar, smoothed out my infelicities, and made the entire book flow better. She is a master at what she does.

Dorothy Smith has vast experience at book layout and always does an excellent job. Her aesthetics are unfailing.

Our daughter, Melissa Holden, a superb artist and designer, produced the unique, eye-catching cover. I loved working with her and viewing her creativity up close.

While speaking of family, I wish to thank our son, Miles, Melissa, and each of their families for their love and help in keeping Mary and me sane during the pandemic. They are a joy to us.

I am greatly indebted to Paul Chutkow, my editor, publisher through Val de Grace Books, and friend for many years for his unceasing encouragement, terrific suggestions, and cogent remarks. There would be no book without him.

Mary, my wife and life's partner for more than fifty years, has always been my first reader and infinitely more.

—ABOUT THE AUTHOR—

Jim Holden has been enchanted by the singular history, natural beauty, and astounding stories of the greater Bay Area, California, and the Western states for more than 50 years. He relishes hiking, travel, and nature. His previous book, *It Happened in Marin*, was a local best seller. He lives with his wife Mary in San Rafael, California.